*no. 19 in a series of research reports
sponsored by the NCTE Committee
on Research

Child and Tale:

*The Origins of Interest

By F. ANDRÉ FAVAT
Northeastern University

 National Council of Teachers of English
1111 Kenyon Road, Urbana, Illinois 61801

Library of Congress Cataloging in Publication Data

Favat, F   André.
    Child and tale.

    (Research report - National Council of Teachers of English ; no. 19)
    Bibliography: p.
    1. Folk-lore and children. 2. Fairy tales—History and criticism. 3. Child psychology.
4. Piaget, Jean, 1896-   I. Title. II. Series: National Council of Teachers of English. Research ; no. 19.
PE1011.N295 no. 19 [GR43.C4] 428'.007s [398'.042]
ISBN 0-8141-0595-5   77-6698

National Council of Teachers of English
Research Report No. 19

People who examine an area of knowledge or a vexing problem from a different perspective and produce new order or clarity as a result merit the recognition and gratitude of their peers. The late Andre Favat was such a person. He took the old question of children's reading interests and reconsidered it within the context of fairy tales and children 6 to 8 years of age. He examined the interest phenomenon itself by seeking to establish the precise intersection of the characteristics of the reader and the characteristics of the tale, that point where interest occurs. Favat's work is fresh and different because of both the type and specificity of analyses he used.

While others have accounted for children's reading interests by pointing to certain psychological characteristics, Favat's work offers new insights to teachers and researchers because of the care with which he established his construct and examined alternative views. Posing the question "What is it about the reader and the book [or story] that causes interest?" Favat proceeds to analyze meticulously the two sources of data to find where common characteristics conjoin. To establish children's psychological characteristics, he draws primarily on Piaget's early work, but only after reviewing criticisms surrounding the work and considering other psychological positions, notably those of Jung and Bettelheim.

The literary content chosen for analysis includes the fairy tales written and collected by Andersen, Perrault, and the Grimms. To ascertain their precise characteristics, Favat chose Propp's *Morphology of the Folktale*, which enabled him to identify the functional components of the stories and their relationships to each other and to the whole. By boldly utilizing Piagetian insights about children and skillfully applying Propp's analyses to the stories, Favat was able to conclude that the tales "embody an accurate representation of the child's conception of the world." He makes these correspondences particularly in regard to the child's egocentrism and conceptions of animism, causality magic, and certain aspects of morality.

The Proppian scheme allowed the investigator to identify not only the nature of events or actions in the tales, but also the pattern and sequence in which they occurred. These factors permitted him to infer a different and exceedingly crucial relationship between child and fairy tales based on the fact that the tales are predictable. "Children soon learn that because tales have certain similarities they can expect, having had a kind of experience with one tale, to have a similar experience with another." Such an inference is in keeping with a psycholinguistic view of reading which characterizes the reader as holding expectations for the material, making predictions, and gaining power in reading as predictions are verified.

Favat provides a different structure for viewing children's interests in *one* genre of literature; however, the model is applicable to other forms of stories and groups of readers. The structure offers teachers a unique way to think about and plan literature experiences for children. If Favat is right, they will be better able to tell children what a book is in fact about. He insightfully warns, however, that the model set forth is for teachers' knowledge—"a reservoir of insight"—not children's lessons.

The monograph may serve equally well as a reservoir of insight for research questions and further theoretical work in children's literature.

Martha L. King
For the NCTE Committee on Research

ACKNOWLEDGMENTS

It is a fortunate researcher whose work has had the benefit of the wise and caring influence of others.

Jeanne Chall, Max Bluestone, Peter Neumeyer, Palmer Czmanske, Allan Ellis, Frank Marsh, and Mary Lee either drew me into the study of children and books or kept me there through their steady interest in me and my work. Maurice Belanger, Barbara Leondar, Steve Lewers, Tove Gerson, Floyd Barbour, and Sarah Eddy listened with special patience at various stages of this study's development. Janet Emig and Pose Lamb encouraged me to seek a wider audience.

Erik Roth struggled to convince me that it was sufficient to wander through the world of the fairy tales, full of wonder but not inquiry. My education taught me differently, and so I set out on this exploration. Now that I am returning, it is important that he recognizes that although there is much information here, my wonder is still none the less.

My parents provided the wellsprings of my subject, then as now, so deeply felt. My father valued books greatly; my mother read to my sister and me and told us never-ending stories of her own invention. They may be surprised, but I hope pleased, to see how far from the source these waters have run.

TABLE OF CONTENTS

INTRODUCTION

When I was very young, I counted among my childhood books companion volumes of stories. One of these books—the one that I seldom turned to—was a book of art stories. Inside were *Black Beauty*, *Heidi*, and *Hans Brinker*, all of which, I realize now, were inventions of writers-for-children. The other book was a different matter altogether. It was a book of fairy tales, and inside was that other world, east of the sun, west of the moon, ruled by testy kings and kind queens, or kind kings and petulant queens, or—pity the rest of the kingdom—testy kings and petulant queens. Here was the great forest that surrounded the castle, enveloped Hansel and Gretel, and harbored the witch; here were the Rapunzels and Rumplestiltskins caught in a swirl of Manichaean forces; here were the princes and merchants' sons who, in the face of every adversity, climbed the glass mountain, and passed through parting hedges.

In less innocent years, I learned that my preference for fairy tales rather than art stories was not peculiar to me alone, but instead was common to most children. I was not able to learn, however, the causes of such intense interest. Feeling that it was not unimportant to know, I mounted this investigation.

To determine the precise configuration of children's early reading interests, the first chapter reviews relevant statements found in essays and anthologies relating to children's books and examines the findings of empirical investigators of children's reading interests. While the conclusions of these descriptions will not achieve unqualified acceptance, they are as precise as the elusive subject and disparate research will allow and do provide the point from which an analytic investigation can proceed. This chapter concludes with establishment of a methodology for analytic studies of reading interests, one based on the careful posing of a question congruent with the nature of the interest phenomenon itself. This question requires for its answer, therefore, precise knowledge of the characteristics of the reader and the book, and a precise explanation of how these characteristics conjoin to produce interest.

The second chapter establishes the literary and psychological reservoirs which will be used throughout. For the literary reservoir, the fairy tales in the European tradition collected or written by Charles Perrault, Jacob and Wilhelm Grimm, and Hans Christian Andersen have been chosen, since they are the fairy tales most available to children today and, indeed, have been for generations. Even this limited reservoir is somewhat diffuse, and so certain distinctions between the tales have been made. For the psychological reservoir, the early work of Jean Piaget has been chosen, since it provides a body of hypotheses and data about children which is significant both in its own right and in its applicability to the present investigation. For various reasons, Piaget's early work has long been criticized, and so an inspection of some of its strengths and weaknesses has been included.

With these literary and psychological reservoirs established, the third chapter analyzes the characteristics of the two major agents—children and fairy tales—which figure in the phenomenon of reading interest under investigation. As the chapter progresses, it becomes clear that there are many similarities between the characteristics of children and the characteristics of fairy tales, similarities so precise they compel the conclusion that the tales embody an accurate representation of the child's conception of the world.

The fourth chapter, drawing upon all that preceded it and in particular the correspondences shown to exist between the child's mind and the fairy tale's construction, considers a number of alternative explanations for children's interest in the tale, and then establishes the present explanation. Any explanation of what occurs in that realm formed by the child's mind and the tale's construction is filled with peril—but it is offered in the hope that it has, at least, good sense. As Coleridge, speaking of poetry, said: " . . . but it must be good sense at all events; just as a palace is more than a house, but it must be a house, at least." This chapter also explores the relationship between the child and the content and form of the fairy tale and accounts not only for the emergence of the child's interest in the tale, but also for its decline and later reappearance.

The final chapter traces implications that the present explanation has for teachers and parents as well as for future researchers. Some of these implications involve the ways in which children receive the tales and respond to them, some involve possible objections to the tales as reading fare for children, and still others involve studying children's reading interests either descriptively or analytically. All are linked, however, by the conviction that we must ensure that our efforts will enable children to find in the stories they read a fulfillment of their own needs and desires.

CHAPTER ONE

CHILDREN'S INTEREST IN FAIRY TALES:
DESCRIPTIVE FINDINGS
AND ANALYTIC METHODOLOGIES

Research in the area of children's reading interests consists of two kinds of studies: *descriptive*, which seek to list *what* it is that children are interested in reading, and *analytic*, which seek to explain *why* children are interested in a particular kind of reading. The present investigation, drawing upon the findings of certain descriptive studies about children's interest in fairy tales, is an analytic study which attempts to discover the reasons for children's interest in fairy tales. In the process, it both examines the problems involved in studying children's reading interests and suggests a methodology for future analytic studies.

The Descriptive Findings

Those concerned with matching children with books will find an imposing array of opinion about what books interest children most, and at what ages. In no case is this more true than in that of the fairy tale, where we consistently find that the essayists and anthologists of children's literature as well as empirical investigators nearly always comment on the relationship between children and the fairy tale.

Essays, anthologies, and booklists. Becker (1947), for instance, speaks of the "omnivorous quality of children's fairy tale hunger" (p. 50), while Hadas (1962) observes that "children are clearly demanding the tales" (p. 11), Cass (1967) finds that "children enjoy [fairy tales] tremendously and ask for them again and again" (p. 28), and Arbuthnot and Sutherland (1972) remark, "for generation after generation, folk tales have continued to be popular with children. Modern youngsters, surrounded by the mechanical gadgets and scientific wonders of our age, are still spellbound by their magic" (p. 151). Though it is sometimes necessary to reconcile the generally approving stance of these writers with their frequent misgivings about possible harm from reading the tales, there is obvious agreement among them that fairy tales greatly interest children.

Such agreement is not so immediately obvious on the matter of the age level when this interest occurs. Becker states that most children "listen . . . to fairy stories as soon as they will listen to anything" (p. 48), and Cass maintains, "children of five or so are ready and eager for the enrichment that the fairy story, folk tale, or simple myth can provide" (p. 28). Arbuthnot and Sutherland reject this early age, however, as being too young (p. 696), and along with Hadas (p. 13), as well as Frank (1941, p. 46) and Larrick (1960, p. 53), suggest 7, 8, or 9 years old.

On the other hand, if the number of books recommended for a particular age group is any indication, the various booklists imply that a later age is when children are interested in fairy tales. For instance, Hadas lists forty-two of sixty-two books of fairy tales for 10, 11, and 12 year olds; Eaton (1957) lists most fairy tales for ages 8 to 13, with the peak number indicated for children between the ages of 10 and 12; and of the fifty books of fairy tales included in Eakin (1962) seven are considered appropriate for the 7 to 9 year olds while the other forty-three are listed for 10 to 12 year olds.

The reason for the disparity between these positions becomes clear upon closer inspection of their different emphases. Becker and Cass, for instance, focus on the child and his cognitive and emotional readiness at various age levels, their concern being not so much with the books children read and enjoy independently, but with the books they could enjoy being read to them. As a result, these two writers find that children of pre-reading age who have fairy tales read to them demonstrate marked interest in this type of story. Arbuthnot and Sutherland, Hadas, Frank, and Larrick also take reading to children into account, but they focus more on the child's independent reading of books. When children's having mastered some of the mechanical tasks of reading is made a condition for their exposure to fairy tales, the suggested age level is naturally higher. When the focus is entirely on books the child can read independently, as in Eaton's and Eakin's compilations, the lists reflect the level of difficulty of the books that the publishers produce, and not the age at which fairy tales are interesting to children. As Eakin states:

> The difficulty level was obtained through a careful, thorough reading of the books, taking into consideration such factors as length and complexity of sentences, kinds of words used, difficulty of concepts and ideas, clarity of presentation of concepts and ideas, and organization of material. (p. xii)

Some consideration, of course, is given to the age group that would be interested in these stories, but the fact remains that these booklists indicate primarily the age at which children would be *able* to read the published books of fairy tales rather than the age at which they would *want* to read them.

To the degree that they focus differently on children or books, and to the degree that independent reading is a factor in the relationship between the two, these guides to children's literature are not always comparable. They do give some indication, however, of children's reading interests, and we can conclude from them that children are interested in the fairy tale and that this interest apparently begins at an early, pre-reading age and continues to approximately ages 9 through 11.

Empirical investigations. The more empirical descriptions of children's reading interests also present the problem of comparability. Varying widely in the methods by which the reservoirs of reading materials are constructed and in the methods by which children's indications of interest are collected, these studies are so diverse that useful generalizations based on their collective findings are difficult to make.[1] Yet, with regard to fairy tales, a number of these investigations over the last 50 years have shown not only that children are interested in fairy tales, but also that children are interested in them only during specific periods of their childhood.

Uhl (1921), for example, showed that of the eleven qualities that teachers and children indicated as having high interest potential in the reading selections presented, the factor of *fancy* or *supernatural*, as found in fairy tales, ranked highest between the ages of 7 and 8, and lowest between the ages of 10 and 12, while at the same time the factor of *reality*, as found in stories of home and child life, ranked lowest between the ages of 7 and 8 and highest between the ages of 10 and 12.

From the work of Washburne and Vogel (1926a) it is possible to discern a pattern of children's interest in fairy tales by examining the frequency with which books containing these stories appear at different age levels. Of the first fifteen most widely read and liked books in grade 4, five are fairy tales; in grade 5, eight of the fifteen are fairy tales; in grade 6, five; and in grade 7, only one.

Terman and Lima (1931) found in their important study that in

---

[1]A detailed examination of some of the methodological considerations involved in empirical descriptive investigations of children's reading interests will be found in Appendix A.

children before 5 years of age, there is an interest in the talking-beast type of nature and animal story, as well as in simple fairy tales. Children of 6 and 7 have as their chief reading interest the nature story, and enjoy having fairy tales read to them. At 8 years, children show the greatest interest in fairy tales. The authors note, "In some children the interest in fairy tales begins at 7 years, in others, not until 9; but with the greatest majority it reaches its maximum at 8 years" (p. 45). They also point out that this interest is practically universal with children:

> From England, France, Germany, Scandinavia, and Italy, in-vestigators report this same thing. Walter Quast reporting a re-cent reading study in Germany says: "By the end of this period (the eighth year), we see the child living enthralled [by] fairy tale literature . . . . This attitude and feeling toward the fairy world is usually abandoned in the ninth or tenth year." (p. 45)

The age of 8 also begins the interest in stories of real life, which continues to grow through the ninth year, and at 10 years there is a marked falling off of interest in fairy tales, while travel stories, biographies, and stories of heroes become popular.

Norvell (1958) produced scores for twenty fairy tales at the elementary and junior-high levels and showed that this type of story is at its highest level of popularity at grade 3, continues to be well liked in grades 4 to 6, but declines in interest in grades 7 to 9. Five tales tested at the senior high-school level showed continued decline (p. 128).

Rogers and Robinson (1963) showed that while first graders ap-peared to have a wide variety of likes, they ranked first such fairy-tale items as "an animal who could talk," "a prince and princess," and "a magic ring"; they ranked last such real-world items as "what an astronaut does," "a person on TV," and "building a bridge" (p. 709).

It is probable that neither these findings nor the findings of other similar investigations which are in agreement, such as Huber (1928), Jordan (1926), Rankin (1944), and Collier and Gaier (1958, 1959), nor the statements of the essayists and anthologists will achieve unqualified acceptance, but these efforts at determin-ing children's reading interests do in various ways confirm one another, and have sufficient strength to warrant some general con-clusions:

1. Children between the ages of 5 and 10 or grades K and 5, whether they select books voluntarily, or are presented with

books and asked for their opinion, express interest in the fairy tale.

2. This interest follows what might be called a *curve of reading preference*; that is, children's interest in fairy tales emerges at a pre-reading age and gradually rises to a peak of interest between the approximate ages of 6 and 8, and then gradually declines to a point of non-interest by the ages of 10 or 11.

3. Concurrent with this decline in interest in the fairy tale, there is an emergence of interest in stories of reality.

These descriptive conclusions, while general, are at the same time as precise as the elusiveness of the subject and the disparateness of the research will allow. They are also precise enough to point the way to an analytic investigation. Having determined that children's interest in fairy tales does exist, and exists with varying intensity at different ages, it seems important that this description be complemented with an analysis of the reasons for this interest and its changes.

A Methodology for Analytic Investigations

Whenever an observation is made that a reader is interested in a particular book, one of two questions usually comes to mind: "What is it about this book that makes it so interesting to this reader?" or, "What is it about this reader that makes him so interested in this book?"

Unfortunately, neither of these questions is likely to yield a satisfying answer because, by focusing on the characteristics of either the reader or the book as being the cause of interest, neither question takes into account what may truly be the case about the origins of reading interest: it is the *conjunction* of the characteristics of the reader and the characteristics of the book that produces the phenomenon of interest. This point would seem to be so obvious that it need not even be mentioned, yet the fact is that those whose subject is readers and books invariably attend either to reader *or* book rather than to *both* reader and book.

Investigators whose focus is on the characteristics of the book draw upon a reservoir of literary knowledge, giving insufficient attention to the characteristics of the reader. Investigators whose focus is on the characteristics of the reader draw primarily upon a reservoir of psychological knowledge, giving insufficient attention to the characteristics of the book. Each focus leads to a truncated methodology with truncated conclusions, because neither leads to a methodology that sufficiently investigates the interest phenomenon as a function of the interaction of reader and book.

The question which would indeed lead to such a methodology which should be asked in such investigations, is "What is it about both this reader and this book, when they come together, that causes interest to occur?" A moment's reflection will show that this question is discriminably different and has the potential for enabling investigators to construct a methodology which ensures examination of both the characteristics of the book, as well as the interaction of these characteristics, thereby bringing about a research methodology consistent with the phenomenon of interest itself.

For the present investigation, therefore, the question that arises from the descriptive studies and their observations about children's interest in fairy tales should be couched as, "What is it about both children and fairy tales, when they come together at some times and not others, that causes interest to occur?" It is this question which determines the methodology of this investigation and which the following chapters attempt to answer.

CHAPTER TWO

ESTABLISHING LITERARY AND PSYCHOLOGICAL RESERVOIRS

As the previous chapter implied, answering the question, "What is it about both children and fairy tales, when they come together at some times and not others, that causes interest to occur?" will require, among other things, psychological knowledge of the characteristics of children and literary knowledge of the characteristics of the tales. This chapter, therefore, will be devoted to delineating the reservoir of literary and psychological knowledge.

The Literary Reservoir:
The Fairy Tales of Perrault, the Grimms, and Andersen

Definitions of the various forms, such as "hero tale," "animal story," "fable," "legend," and the like, which Thompson (1946) indicates comprise the vast category, "traditional prose tales" (p. 7ff.) leads us into confusion, since the characteristics of one form are to be found among the characteristics of another. Animals, after all, exist not only in "animal stories" but in "hero tales" and "fables" as well. Heroes exist not only in "hero stories" but in "legends," and so on. The term "fairy tale" is no less elusive, but is more easily defined because it has received careful attention. A fairy tale, it is generally agreed, is a folk tale, but not all folk tales are fairy tales. A folk tale involves an unvarying sequence of a limited number of possible episodes (thus distinguishing it from all other narratives), occurs in a world without definite locality (thus distinguishing it from local legends), and is characterized by magical happenings, but not by gods or demigods (thus distinguishing it from myths) (cf. Thompson, p. 8; David and David 1964, p. ix ff.; Brereton 1957, p. x). A definition of "fairy tale" can be supported with examples known to most readers. A fairy tale is a story such as "Cinderella," "Snow White," or "Hansel and Gretel." A fairy tale is *not* a story such as "Goldilocks and the Three Bears," "Little Red Riding Hood," or "The Three Little Pigs," stories which, although they are commonly and loosely referred to as fairy tales, do not in fact possess an unvarying sequence of episodes or deeply magical happenings.

The number of stories that can be called "fairy tales" is overwhelming. Determining which are most frequently available to children—that is, determining what shall be the reservoir of stories for the present investigation—leaves us farther from certainty than we ought to be. Ordinarily, a frequency count of the stories to which children have greatest access would result in a reasonable reservoir. A moment's reflection shows, however, that children can come upon fairy tales in a multitude of ways. Basal readers, trade books, adult storytelling, and dramatizations (either actual or animated) all offer children opportunities to read or hear fairy tales. With sources so multiple and so ephemeral, a frequency count is not likely to produce a reservoir that very accurately represents the fairy tales to which children have the greatest access.

General observation, however, does show that most of the fairy tales available to children are those which have been collected or written in French by Charles Perrault, in German by Jacob and Wilhelm Grimm, and in Danish by Hans Christian Andersen. Publishers' search for variety and the increased awareness of cultural relativity have made a number of American Indian, African, East Indian and other such tales available to children. These are seldom fairy tales as defined above, however, and in any event, they have not displaced the stories of Perrault, the Grimms, and Andersen, which still account for most of the fairy tales children encounter.

The tales of Charles Perrault. Perrault's *Histoire du contest du temps passé avec des moralités*, more generally known as *Contes de ma mère l'Oye*,[1] was first published in 1697, and may have had its origins in Perrault's first-hand knowledge of the popular tradition, or in his second-hand knowledge of that tradition through the stories written in Italian in 1550 by Francesco Straparola in his *Piacevoli notti*. Or perhaps, if he understood the difficult Neapolitan dialect, Perrault had read Giambatista Basile's ribald *Pentamerone*, published in 1634-1636.

Regardless of Perrault's sources, it is obvious to readers having even a modest acquaintance with folk literature that he must have subjected the original stories to certain transformations that pro-

---

[1] The edition used is: Geoffrey Brereton, trans. and ed., *The Fairy Tales of Charles Perrault* (Baltimore: Penguin Books, 1957).

duced the distinctive tone of these "bagatelles," as he called them. In the stories there is the sense, for instance, of a frivolity that relishes occasional asides to the audience. When the ogre's wife in "Hop O' My Thumb," for instance, discovers her seven daughters swimming in blood with their throats mistakenly cut by the ogre, Perrault observes, "She began by fainting, which is the first resource of most women in such circumstances." The audience, as implied by the woodcut illustrations in the early editions depicting Mother Goose with children by her side, would seem to be these *naifs*, but reference to the stories themselves hardly supports such a view. Instead, the intended audience must surely have been quite knowing in the ways of the world, much the same, one suspects, as the author himself. "Hop O' My Thumb" again provides an example. Aided by his purloined seven-league boots, Hop O' My Thumb enters the king's service by carrying orders to the army. But he also carries news for the ladies of the court. Perrault observes that, while a vast number of these ladies gave Hop O' My Thumb anything he wished for news of their lovers, only a few gave him letters to take to their husbands—and in these cases they paid rather badly.

Perrault was probably not attempting to give a faithful picture of his period. But even though geography and historical time are vague, the stories are filled with an unmistakable sense of the life and fashion of the day. When the prince enters the palace wherein lies Sleeping Beauty, he goes through courtyards and rooms similar to those of Versailles, including the Cour de Marbre, the Chambre du Roi, and most specifically the Galerie des Glaces, which, if they are familiar to readers today, must have been commonplace to readers in the Court of Louis XIV (Perrault, 1956, p. 90).

The tales of Jacob and Wilhelm Grimm. As with Perrault, the Grimms' purpose, in their *Kinder und Hausmärchen*,[2] was not to prepare a volume of stories for children, and they always regretted the title of their collection of stories which appeared in seven editions over nearly fifty years starting in 1812. Unlike Perrault, though, their purpose was serious, and indeed, scholarly: to preserve the *märchen* as far as possible in the form in which they were still being told in the German provinces.

This desire to preserve the oral tradition, however, did not

---

[2]The edition used is: James Stern, ed., and Margaret Hunt, trans., *The Complete Grimm's Fairy Tales* (New York: Pantheon Books, 1944).

mean that the Grimms' stories as published were the same as the Grimms' stories as collected. Tonnelat (1912) shows, for example, that while the Grimms made no changes in the contents of the stories, they effected innumerable stylistic changes from edition to edition, all of which tended to make the stories more coherent, dramatic, and concrete. Different versions of the same story were combined to produce a definitive version, motivation was supplied to the characters where it was lacking, indirect discourse and statements about what the characters thought and did were replaced by dialogue, names were given to certain unnamed characters, and so on. In spite of these changes, however, the Grimms' stories, except where there is an occasional closing formula such as that in "Hansel and Gretel" ("My tale is done; there runs a mouse; whosoever catches it may make himself a big fur cap of it") have little presence of a transforming narrator, and are consistently without definite time or place—characteristics quite the opposite from those of Perrault's stories.

The tales of Hans Christian Andersen. Andersen's fairy tales[3] appeared between 1832 and 1872. Though he initially wrote his stories for children with the intention of "winning the coming generations," by 1843 he had begun to write them with an adult audience in mind, hoping that the adults would have "a little to think about" as they were reading the stories to their children (Larsen 1955, p. 50ff).

Some of Andersen's stories, such as "The Nightingale," "The Emperor's New Clothes," or "The Ugly Duckling," are his original inventions. Though they have a fairy tale atmosphere about them, the kings and the talking animals serve mostly as vehicles for Andersen's social criticism. Indeed, Andersen saw his stories as a means of avenging insults, satirizing follies, and in general giving vent to his bitter struggle to discover where his talents lay and to make them respected by the literary critics of the day (Rubow 1955, p. 122).

Other Andersen stories, such as "The Wild Swans," "The Tinderbox" or "Inchelina," are more closely related to the folk tradition. In outward appearances they resemble the stories found in Perrault and the Grimms, but, as the following analysis will show, while Perrault and the Grimms transmitted their fairy tales essentially as they received them from the popular tradition, making

---

[3]The edition used is: Erik Christian Haugaard, trans., *Hans Christian Andersen: The Complete Fairy Tales and Stories* (Garden City, N. Y.: Doubleday, 1974).

only stylistic changes, Andersen wrought substantial revision and departed often from the tales as received.

Some distinctions between the three collections. Among the many approaches to the study of the various folklore genre, there has been a growing awareness that behind the incidents that occur in a great many stories lies a common pattern. Raglan (1936), for instance, has demonstrated that there is a pattern of 21 possible incidents that usually occur in the lives of such heroes as Oedipus, Moses, Siegfried, and King Arthur. Even though some lives contain more of the incidents than others, the events in the hero's life include most of the following:

> (1) His mother is a royal virgin. (2) His father is a king, and (3) often a near relative of his mother, but (4) the circumstances of his conception are unusual, and (5) he is also reputed to be the son of a god. (6) At birth an attempt is made, often by his father, to kill him, but (7) he is spirited away, and (8) reared by foster parents in a far country. (9) We are told nothing of his childhood, but (10) on reaching manhood he returns or goes to his future kingdom. (11) After victory over the king and/or a giant, dragon, or wild beast, (12) he marries a princess, often the daughter of his predecessor, and (13) becomes king. (14) For a time he reigns uneventfully, and (15) prescribes laws, but (16) later he loses favor with the gods and/or his subjects, and (17) is driven from the throne and city. (18) He meets with a mysterious death, (19) often at the top of a hill. (20) His children, if any, do not succeed him. (21) His body is not buried, but nevertheless he has one or more holy sepulchers. (p. 179ff)

Noting that the incidents fall definitely into three groups—those connected with the hero's birth, those connected with his accession to the throne, and those connected with his death, Raglan shows that the number of these incidents in the story of Oedipus is twenty-two, in the story of Theseus, twenty, and in Arthur, nineteen; Romulus, eighteen; Heracles, seventeen; Perseus, eighteen; Jason, fifteen; Bellerophon, sixteen; Pelops, thirteen; Robin Hood, thirteen; and Siegfried, eleven. It is possible to question some of Raglan's tabulations, but there is no denying that his analysis points to a consistent heroic plot that recurs with remarkable frequency. Nor is Raglan alone in making such observations. Polti (1912), Campbell (1968), and Vries (1963), among others, have produced schemata pointing to definite similarity among incidents found in various stories of the popular tradition.

None of these studies is of greater general import nor of more

use to the present investigation than Propp's *Morfológija skáski*.[4]
In this work, Propp produced a description of the fairy tale according to its component parts and a description of their relationship.
He noticed, for instance, that sets of events such as the following
occurred:

1. A Czar gives an eagle to a hero. The eagle carries the hero
   away to another kingdom.

2. An old man gives Súcenko a horse. The horse carries
   Súcenko away to another kingdom.

3. A sorcerer gives Iván a little boat. The boat takes Iván to
   another kingdom.

4. A princess gives Iván a ring. Young men appearing from out
   of the ring carry Iván away into another kingdom. (p. 19ff)

Observing that both constants and variables were present, Propp
hypothesized that, though the names and attributes of the
dramatis personae change, their actions and functions do not.
Subsequent investigation of 100 Russian fairy tales showed this to
be fact.

Propp found that the characters of different tales often performed the same actions recurring with "astounding" frequency.
He observed that, while the number of personages in the stories
was extremely large, the number of functions was extremely small,
a fact which accounted for the tales' uniformity and repetitiveness
on one hand, and their multiformity and variety on the other.
Propp extracted thirty-one actions or functions that could exist in a
fairy tale, designating them as nouns expressing action. Thus the
action of a villain causing harm or injury to a member of a family is
referred to as "villainy," the hero leaving home is "departure,"
the hero marrying and ascending the throne are "wedding," and
so on. Propp observed that a large number of the functions occurred in pairs, such as the addressing of an interdiction to the
hero and the hero's violation of the interdiction; the pursuit of the
hero and the rescue of the hero from pursuit; the villain's attempts
at deceiving his victim and the victim's unwitting submission to
the deception, and so on. Still other functions occurred in larger

---

[4]The edition used is: Vladimir Propp, *Morphology of The Folktale*, trans. Laurence Scott (Austin, Tex.: University of Texas Press, 1968). A Complete listing of
the thirty-one functions, an understanding of which will be helpful in the remaining discussion of Propp's description of the fairy tale, will be found in Appendix B.

groups, such as the hero's being tested by someone he meets, perhaps an old woman asking for help, his reaction to the test, and his acquiring the use of a magical device or agent.

Propp also noted that although all tales did not possess all thirty-one functions, whatever functions did exist were always in the same sequence. For example, if one imagines the prototypic tale as existing along a continuum such as this:

1 2 3 31

then various individual tales could consist of various numbers of these functions. But those functions that did exist in each tale would always proceed from left to right. Even though certain functions might be absent within a section of the continuum, this would still not change the order of the functions:

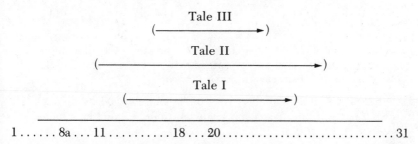

1 ...... 8a ... 11 .... 18 ... 20 31

Propp also showed that not only could his scheme accurately describe Russian fairy tales other than the 100 he examined, but also and more significantly, non-Russian fairy tales. What mattered most was not the particular fairy tale or its country of origin, but the degree to which a particular tale remained true to the folk tradition, uncorrupted by literary influence.

Of the stories in the present reservoir, however, the tales of Perrault and the Grimms do veer widely from Propp's scheme. Even though these stories display a less pure and stable form of the scheme, the scheme is there, and employing it as an analytical device permits useful observations.

Perrault's "The Fairies" exhibits the following pattern:

> The younger, and unfavored, of two daughters is sent by her mother to draw water from the well. (Function 11, *departure*)
>
> At the well, the younger daughter meets a poor woman who asks for a drink of water. (Function 12, *test by the donor*)

The younger daughter willingly gives the woman a drink. (Function 13, *reaction*)

The woman decrees that for every word the younger daughter speaks, either a flower or a precious jewel will fall from her mouth. (Function 14, *receipt of a magical agent*)

Upon the younger daughter's return home, she speaks to her mother, and the flowers and jewels fall from her mouth. (Function 17, *branding*)

[At this point the story repeats itself, this time involving the elder, and favored, daughter.]

The mother sends her elder daughter to the well. (Function 11, *departure*)

The elder daughter meets the poor woman, now magnificently dressed, who asks again for a drink of water. (Function 12, *test by the donor*)

The elder daughter saucily refuses to give the woman a drink. (Function 13, *reaction*)

The woman decrees that for every word the elder daughter speaks, either a snake or a toad will fall from her mouth. (Function 14, *receipt of a magical agent*)

Upon the elder daughter's return home, she speaks to her mother and the snakes and toads fall from her mouth. (Function 17, *branding*)

[After this first contrastive repetition, the story returns to the younger daughter.]

The mother blames the younger daughter for her older daughter's plight, and chases the younger daughter into the forest. (Function 21, *pursuit*)

A king's son comes upon the younger daughter in the forest and speaks to her. (Function 22, *rescue*)

The younger daughter responds, and the king's son sees flowers and jewels fall from her mouth. (Function 27, *recognition*)

The king's son takes the younger daughter to the palace and marries her. (Function 31, *wedding*)

[At this point, the story repeats itself again, with the second contrastive repetition.]

Unable to live with her snake- and toad-spewing elder daughter, the mother chases her into the forest. (Function 21, *pursuit*)

No one will take the elder daughter in because they see the
snakes and toads falling from her mouth. (Assimilation of
Function 22, *rescue*, and Function 27, *recognition*)

The point here is not so much that Perrault's tale adheres to
Propp's scheme, which it does, but rather that the application of
Propp's scheme to the tale lays bare its essential features. The
logical relationships of the events are consistent, each event ar-
ticulating precisely with the others: being sent to the well enables
the younger daughter to meet the poor woman, which enables the
poor woman to test the daughter, which enables her to respond,
and so on; the mother's chasing of the younger daughter into the
forest enables the king's son to come upon her, which enables him
to recognize her state of enchantment, and so on. The aesthetic
relationships are similarly precise and are characterized by patterned contrastive repetitions at all levels: the good younger
daughter goes to the well and returns with the gift of flowers and
jewels, while the evil elder daughter goes to the well and returns
with the curse of snakes and toads; the younger daughter flees to
the woods where she is rescued by the prince, while the elder
daughter flees to the woods and is abandoned by all, and so on.
The moral order exhibited by the relationships of the events is
similar: the essential goodness of the younger daughter is rewarded, while the essential wickedness of the elder daughter is
punished.

Applying Proppian analysis to the stories in the Grimms' collection produces similar results, even with different patterns of plot,
one of which is found in "The Goose Girl":

> The princess, accompanied by her maid-in-waiting, departs for
> the kingdom of the prince to whom she is betrothed. (Func-
> tion 1, *absentation*)

> The princess's mother gives her a handkerchief which she
> tells the princess to preserve carefully. (Function 2, *interdic-
> tion*)

> Along the way, the maid-in-waiting refuses to dismount to get
> the princess a cup of water from a stream, so the princess dis-
> mounts, and in stooping over the stream, drops the handker-
> chief, which then floats away. (Assimilation of Function 3, *vio-
> lation*, with Function 6, *trickery*, and Function 7, *complicity*)

> The maid-in-waiting forces the princess, now powerless, to
> change places with her, and to swear that she will not reveal
> her plight to any person at the court. (Function 8, *villainy*)

The princess arrives at her betrothed's castle clothed in the garments of the maid-in-waiting and is sent out to become a goose girl. (Function 23, *unrecognized arrival*)

The maid-in-waiting arrives at the castle clothed in the garments of the princess and is welcomed into the court as a princess. (Function 24, *unfounded claim*)

[At this point, there are added scenes, omitted here, of the princess as goose girl.]

The prince's father, the old king, suspecting that the beautiful goose girl is more than a goose girl, charges her to tell him the truth, which she has sworn not to tell any person. (Function 25, *difficult task*)

The princess creeps into an iron stove and tells her story to the stove. (Function 26, *solution*)

The king hears the story through the pipe in the stove, and learns that the goose girl is the real princess and that the maid-in-waiting is posing as the princess. (Assimilation of Function 27, *recognition*, and Function 28, *exposure*)

The princess is dressed in royal garments. (Function 29, *transfiguration*)

The maid-in-waiting, in answering a riddle which the king poses to her, pronounces her own death sentence. (Function 30, *punishment*)

The prince and princess are married and reign over the kingdom. (Function 31, *wedding*)

That the logical, aesthetic, and moral relationships in the Grimms' story exist with the same precision as those in Perrault's story is obvious. When the princess violates her mother's interdiction, she becomes powerless, logically preparing the way for the maid-in-waiting to seize control over her. Changing from the clothes of a princess to the clothes of a servant in the beginning of the story is aesthetically balanced with changing from the clothes of a servant to the clothes of a princess at the end of the story; by speaking, the princess achieves her salvation, and by speaking, the maid-in-waiting pronounces her own doom. Morally, the essential goodness of the princess is rewarded, and the essential wickedness of the maid-in-waiting is punished.

Such precise relationships are not to be found, however, in the tales of Andersen. For example, in his "The Tinderbox":

A soldier is on his way home from the wars. (This would appear to be Function 11, *departure*, but departures in Perrault and the Grimms are always departures *from* home and not departures *for* home.)

Along the way, the soldier meets an old witch who asks him to retrieve her tinderbox from inside a hollow tree, for which he may keep the money he finds there. (This would appear to be Function 12, *test by the donor*, but donors in Perrault and the Grimms establish the test of the hero without giving any indication that the hero will be rewarded by his right performance.)

The soldier retrieves the tinderbox and the money. (Function 13, *reaction*)

When he is safely out of the hollow tree, the soldier refuses to give the tinderbox to the witch, cuts off her head, and goes off with both money and tinderbox. (This would appear to be Function 14, *receipt of the magical agent*, but in Perrault and the Grimms, the hero receives, but does not steal, the magical agent, and does not kill the donor.

In "The Swineherd":

The prince, though poor, sets out to win the hand of the Emperor's daughter. (Assimilation of Function 8a, *lack*, and Function 11, *departure*)

The prince presents the princess with a rose which grew on his father's grave, as well as a nightingale, and later tries to woo her with a rattle and a singing pot which he has made. (These would appear to be magical agents, but unlike the magical agents in Perrault and the Grimms, they do not come to the hero through Functions 7 and 8, *test by the donor* and *reaction*, but instead are already his own possessions, or in the case of the pot and the rattle, objects which he himself has fashioned.)

In "The Flying Trunk":

The spendthrift merchant's son has nothing left to his name except four shillings, a pair of old slippers, and an old dressing gown. (Function 8a, *lack*)

A friend gives him a trunk that can fly. (This would appear to be Function 14, *receipt of magical agent*, but again, the hero does not earn it through Function 7, *test by the donor* and Function 8, *reaction*)

The merchant's son flies to the land of the Turks. (Function 15, *spatial transference*)

The merchant's son must tell a story to the sultan and sultana
in order to win their daughter's hand. (Function 25, *difficult
task*)

The merchant's son tells his story and the sultan and sultana
are much pleased. (Function 26, *solution*)

[At this point, Function 31, *wedding*, would be expected to
appear, but instead, the merchant's son, as a treat for the sultan's populace, places fireworks in his trunk, and meteor-like,
flies away. In the process, the fireworks ignite the trunk,
which burns to ashes, leaving the merchant's son unable to
return for the princess and their wedding.]

This imprecision of the relationship among events also means
that in Andersen's stories there is not the clear indication of each
character's fate found in Perrault and the Grimms, where the end
of the story allows no irresolution: no wicked stepmother is left
unpunished, no faithful servant, good brother, or kind prince is
left unrewarded. But in Andersen, the white butterfly who helps
Inchelina to sail across the brook is left tied to a leaf, and it is
never known what becomes of it; similarly, the princess in "The
Flying Trunk" may or may not still be waiting for the merchant's
son to return for her. Even when the resolution is indicated in
Andersen, it does not necessarily grow out of a morality such as
that in Perrault and the Grimms—where justice comes in the form
of reward for virtue and punishment for evil—in "The Tinderbox," for example, the soldier kills the witch, who has done no
evil and who in fact has shown him kindness.

Moreover, although the stories of all three collections show the
hero struggling against the powers of evil or the rigors of depriva-
tion, in Perrault and the Grimms the hero is invariably aided by
chance; that is, he comes upon a person or animal of magical powers from whom, as a reward for some good deed, he receives a
magical device which enables him to make his fortune. For the
worthy hero, the donor always has good intentions, but an un-
worthy hero invariably comes upon a donor who has evil intentions, and who strikes a bargain with him and presents him with a
gift or service that ultimately ensnares and disables. The bargain
brings immediate pleasure, but eventually causes the hero to
come to grief. The Grimms' "Rapunzel" and "Rumplestiltskin"
are prototypic tales of this latter sort.

In the stories of Andersen, even though magical devices do in
fact figure prominently in the action, so does the force of Provi-
dence as the protector and enabler of the elect. In "The Wild

Swans," Elisa wanders through woods in search of her enchanted brothers:

> She thought about her brothers, and trusted that God would
> not leave her. There ahead of her was a wild apple tree.
> Hadn't God let it grow there so that the hungry could eat?
> (Haugaard, p. 120)

and later when she rests in the darkness of night:

> When she lay down to sleep she was hopelessly sad; but then
> the branches above her seemed to be drawn aside like a cur-
> tain, and she saw God looking down at her, with angels peep-
> ing over His shoulders and out from under His arms. And in
> the morning when she awoke, she did not know [whether] she
> had really seen God or whether it had merely been a dream.
> (Haugaard, p. 120-121)

The case is of course overstated because references to Providential intervention exist in the Grimms' stories as well. For example,
in "The Pink," the queen prays for a child, and an angel brings
her the news that her prayers will be answered; later, as she lies
imprisoned and dying, the queen confidently recites: "The gra-
cious and merciful God who has supported me in the tower will
soon set me free" (Stern, p. 360). But such occurrences are exceptional, and so the distinction made above is generally an accurate
one. Providential intervention is by no means so near the surface
in Perrault and the Grimms as it is in the stories of Andersen.

Finally, the laws of relationship which apply to one story in Perrault and the Grimms apply to all the stories in their collections,
whereas in Andersen it is not possible to generalize from the laws
of relationship in one story to the laws of relationship in others.
Expectations which are always fulfilled in Perrault and the
Grimms are not necessarily fulfilled in Andersen. A prince in Andersen may successfully perform a difficult task and win the princess in one story, but this does not assure that another prince in
another Andersen story will come to similar good fortune.

And yet in spite of these crucial differences, there is the unmistakable sense that the stories in these three collections are all of
one kind. The reason is this: although the relationships that exist
between the various actions of the characters in the stories of Perrault and the Grimms are different from those in Andersen, the
actions themselves, as well as the types of characters, are the same
in all three collections. Thus, although in Perrault and the Grimms
a prince's successful performance of difficult tasks with the aid of
magical agents will inevitably produce the prince's wedding with

a princess and although in Andersen such predictability is never
assured, the fact still remains that the Andersen stories contain the
tasks themselves, as well as princes and donors, magical agents,
princesses, and the like, that are to be found in Perrault and the
Grimms. It is the presence of these elements, distributed equally
among all three collections, that produces this sense of identity,
however mistaken, and that obscures the fundamental distinctions.

The Psychological Reservoir: The Early Work of Jean Piaget

Having established a reservoir from which knowledge about
fairy tales can be drawn, it remains to do the same for a reservoir
which can provide knowledge about children. Establishing this
reservoir, however, is easier. Few would deny that there is any
greater body of hypotheses and data about children than that
which comprises the work of Jean Piaget. As will become apparent, there is no part of Piaget's work more relevant to the present
investigation than his early work, and in particular, *The Language
and Thought of the Child* (1955), *Judgment and Reasoning in the
Child* (1968), *The Child's Conception of the World* (1967), and
The Moral Judgment of the Child (1965).

Piaget has been most often criticized for this early work, with its
subjective clinical procedures, paucity of statistical evidence, and
diffuse reporting. Validation studies have confirmed the early
findings, and the respectability and acceptance accorded to
Piaget's later work have been applied to his early work as well.
But because there are lingering doubts about the early investigations, reference to and application of them must still be accom-
panied by some examination of their strengths and weaknesses.
Without exploring every aspect of relevant criticism, it is possible
to indicate at least two aspects of Piaget's early work to which
there has been typical and full critical reaction, aspects which will
figure importantly in later chapters.

The studies of animism. There has been much discussion of
Piaget's hypotheses about children's animist beliefs. Huang (1943)
provided an extensive examination of the literature on animism in
children and concluded that research had not supported Piaget's
hypothesis that young children endow objects with feelings and
consciousness. Huang proposed that the young child's lack of understanding of the adult's animate and inanimate dichotomy is due
not to a universal animist cast of mind but to incomplete differentiation: the child gradually moves, by "mutual definition and con-

trast," from a neutral and indeterminate state to a correct grasp of concepts. Huang and Lee (1945) later published an experimental analysis of child animism, complementing Huang's earlier summary. On the basis of the responses from forty Chinese children between the ages of 3 and 8 who were asked about ten objects (dog, tree, river, stone, pencil, bicycle, ball, automobile, watch, and the moon), Huang and Lee concluded that an inanimate object was said to be alive only in a small proportion of cases. Also, the distribution of correct answers among the different objects indicated that animist concepts, where present, were to be explained by the apparent characteristics of the specific object rather than by any general tendency in the children.

Strauss (1951), however, rejected the Huang-Lee conclusions, with astute argumentation and more careful analysis of the Huang-Lee data than Huang and Lee themselves seemed to perform. He showed that these data could just as well be interpreted as supporting Piaget's hypotheses. Strauss observed " . . . we may agree that the data indicate that not all inanimate objects are equally hard to classify correctly, [but] to make this statement is not equivalent to saying that young children do not display a general tendency to endow inanimate objects with life and consciousness" (p. 112).

Klingberg (1957) re-opened the whole matter. Investigating ninety-seven Swedish children between the ages of 7 and 10 with Huang's method, he concluded that the distinction between living and not-living is much better applied at this age than Piaget thought, even though at the age of 9-10 the distinction is difficult with regard to certain objects. Klingberg also concluded that the question of whether the distinctions between living and not-living objects was caused by insufficient knowledge or primitive thinking cannot be resolved through such empirical investigations. He dismissed the whole question because "Piaget is influenced by the recapitulation theory and the doctrine of the primitive mentality of primitive man, theories that have little connection with modern science" (p. 238). However, Klingberg's ascribing to Piaget such recapitulation theory tendencies ignores completely Piaget's own consistent disclaimers:

> The term animism denotes a belief peculiar to primitive peoples. If we use it here in speaking of the child it is as if we were deciding out of hand the question as to whether these similar beliefs were identical for the primitive and the child. But such is not the case. We shall use the word "animism" simply as a generic term, leaving the question open whether

the various types of animism have the same or distinct
psychological origins. (1967, p. 170)

The Huang and Lee-Strauss-Klingberg exchanges, for all their
prominence in the literature, are not unlike receding mirrors.
Whatever contribution they do make is minimized because they
give inadequate attention to Russell's investigations (1940), which
predated the animism controversy by many years and which cannot be ignored.

Using a standardized set of questions adopted from Piaget,
"Does the _____ know where it is? Why? Does the _____
feel when I touch it? Why?" Russell asked 774 children from ages
6 to 15 from varied geographical locations and socio-economic
status to classify 20 objects. Russell concluded that (1) It was possible to classify individuals into the stages of animism suggested
by Piaget, and that this held true for French, American, American
Indian, and even feeble-minded subjects; (2) It was probable that
individuals pass sequentially through the series of concept stages
with increasing mental and chronological age; (3) Although the
fundamental validity of Piaget's classification of concept stages
had been proved, the data revealed the impossibility of limiting
the age range of the stages as Piaget had attempted to do; (4) The
development of animist concepts was very nearly the same for all
groups studied, despite the varied geographic location and socio-
economic status; (5) There were no significant differences in the
development of animist stages between male and female subjects
in any of the groups; and (6) The stages of animism were related to
both mental age and chronological age (p. 364).

Russell's study is valuable not only because it encompasses a
larger and more varied sample in every respect than did Piaget's
limited sample of Swiss children, but also because it adheres
closely to Piaget's own clinical method of questioning while standardizing the questioning procedure to reduce charges of subjec-
tivism. Huang complained that the standardized procedure, by
refusing to follow the child's leads or to vary the questions according to individual circumstances, probably suppressed further responses which might have a disillusioning effect on apparent
interpretations: "In standardizing a technique one facilitates classification of responses by reducing it to a rather mechanical level,
but probably pays the price of oversimplifying inherently compli-
cated phenomena" (p. 105). Few would disagree with Huang, and
yet few would not applaud Russell for having struck a workable
balance, one which achieves a moderate and appropriate control
over the excessively verbal and elusive procedure used by Piaget.

One of Russell's conclusions, that it was impossible to limit the age range of the stages as Piaget did, at first seems to run counter to one of the most significant aspects of Piaget's findings. But closer examination of Piaget's statements shows him admitting that even though children's animist beliefs could be classified into successive stages present at different age levels, each individual child was capable of retrogressive movements in the series of stages, just as much as he was capable of progressing in a straight line. For the individual child, observed Piaget (1967), "animism is always varying and is sometimes more and sometimes less" (p. 188).

The studies of moral development. The orderliness of Piaget's stages was also questioned with regard to children's moral development. In a study of the moral judgment of 244 boys between the ages of 5 and 14, MacRae (1954) tested Piaget's theory that changes with age in answers to certain questions reflected a change from relations of authority to relations of equality. Mac-Rae's conclusion, supported by a great deal of statistical evidence, was that, contrary to what Piaget's theories would indicate, indices of parental discipline and control and internalization of parental requirements did not show a decrease with the subjects' increase in age.

Similarly, after questioning middle-class subjects of three different age groups about the problem of restoring right order in instances of physical aggression between children, Durkin (1959a) found that, though Piaget's contention that a relationship existed between chronological age and justice concepts was substantiated, the acceptance of reciprocity as a justice principle did not increase with age. Durkin (1959b) also found that the oldest children as well as the youngest tended to seek justice in the authority person, which did not support Piaget's notion that acceptance of reciprocity as a justice principle increases with age.

Research into the moral judgment of older children, an aspect to which Piaget gives but scant attention, has tended to support the above conclusion. Loughran (1967), for instance, testing sixty-eight adolescents between the ages of 11 and 18 with moral situation stories similar to Piaget's, found that indeed, as in Piaget's findings, there were three levels of moral judgment—that is, authority, equality, and equity—but that, contrary to Piaget's findings, even adolescents still made their judgments under the moral constraint of authority figures.

The most extensive of these researches have been Kohlberg's. Using a core group of seventy-two boys from three different age groups, 10, 13, 16, from both upper-middle and lower to lower-middle classes, Kohlberg (1963) interviewed the subjects about hypothetical moral dilemmas similar to those Piaget used. The situations were ones in which acts of obedience to legal-social rules or to the commands of authority conflicted with the human needs or welfare of other individuals. Each subject was asked to choose whether one should perform the obedience-serving act or the need-serving act, and was then asked a series of questions probing the thinking underlying his choice. Kohlberg's findings did not support Piaget's notion that there is a general trend of moral development in children that moves from an authoritarian ethic to a democratic ethic, that is, a shift from unilateral respect for adults to a mutual respect for peers. But Kohlberg (1964) came, as did the other researchers above, to support Piaget's notion that the child's earliest morality is oriented to obedience, punishment, and impersonal forces, where judgment is based on immediate, external, physical circumstances, and that this morality progresses toward more subjective and internal values and norms.

The fact that MacRae, Durkin, Loughran, and Kohlberg all found that Piaget's stages of moral development were not inviolable and that in fact many older children demonstrated characteristics of moral judgment similar to those of younger children, at first may seem to discount a most significant aspect of Piaget's work. But again, as with the stages of animism, Piaget (1965) clearly indicates that the various moralities follow upon one another without constituting definite stages: "Though we could not point to any stages properly so-called, which followed one another in a necessary order, we were able to define processes whose final terms were quite distinct from one another. These processes might mingle and overlap more or less in the life of each child, but they marked nevertheless the broad divisions of moral development" (p. 175).

In the final analysis, however, what is essential about these studies is not so much that this or that aspect of Piaget's hypotheses has or has not been supported. Rather it is that, when Piaget's intentions have not been overlooked while seeking the statistical proof of his hypotheses, validation studies have confirmed the general configuration of these hypotheses (cf. Laurendeau and Pinard 1962; Gouin Décarie 1965; Elkind and Flavell 1969). Consequently, Piaget's work can be accepted as invaluable to the present investigation.

CHAPTER THREE

ESTABLISHING CORRESPONDENCES BETWEEN
CHILDREN AND FAIRY TALES

Previous chapters have established the fact that children's interest in fairy tales emerges and declines between the ages of 5 and 10, with the point of highest interest occurring between the ages of 6 and 8; these same chapters have also established the particular reservoirs of literary and psychological information that can now be used in examining the characteristics of the two major agents—children and fairy tales—that figure in this phenomenon of reading interest.[1]

Even for those who have never thought about the matter before, it will soon become apparent, as this chapter progresses, that there are many similarities between the characteristics of children as described by Piaget and the characteristics of the fairy tales of Perrault, the Grimms, and Andersen which form the present reservoir. Closer inspection will show, in fact, that the characteristics of the fairy tales correspond precisely with the characteristics Piaget ascribed to children.

Magical Beliefs in Child and Tale

Magic and the child. In *The Child's Conception of the World* (1967), Piaget uses Levy-Bruhl's term "participation" to describe the relationship that children believe to exist between two beings or objects; that is, children regard beings or objects either as partially identical or as having a direct influence on one another even though there is no spatial contact or intelligible causal connection between them (p. 132). Participation as a characteristic of chil-

---

[1]Throughout this and the remaining chapters, the words "child" and "children" will refer specifically to those between the ages of 6 and 8, and will refer to children in general, ignoring any large departures from type which might result from such influences as environment, race, ability, sex, and the like.

Such departures could be expected to be minimal anyway, for most research shows that at this stage of the child's development, it is age, and not environment, race, ability, or sex that has primary influence on reading interests (cf. Thorndike 1941; Feeley 1974; Zimet and Camp 1974).

dren's thought becomes clearer through reference to what Piaget determined was one of its manifestations, that is, the child's belief in magic, which by Piaget's definition means the use individuals believe they can make of participation in order to modify reality (p. 133). A number of such convictions about magic exist in children. They believe, for instance, in magic by participation between objects; that is, they believe that an object or place can be used to influence another object. Piaget observed that frequently the choice of the magical object seemed to be determined by its resemblance to the object which the child sought to influence. One of Piaget's collaborators, speaking of herself in the third person, reported her own recollection of such childhood belief:

> A little girl of six used to pass often with her governess by a lake where some rare water-lilies grew. Every time she would throw some little stones into the water (always choosing them round and white) and taking care not to be seen by the governess. She thought that the next day water-lilies would appear in the place where the stones had fallen. For this reason, in the hope of thus being able to reach the flowers, she always threw the stones quite near the edge. (1967, p. 143)

Children also believe in magic by participation between actions and things; here children perform some action believing that it exercises, through participation, an influence on a particular event they either desire or fear. The examples of this type of magic are numerous and varied. One of Piaget's collaborators recollects:

> Every evening from about the age of 6 to 8, I was terrified by the idea of not waking up in the morning. I used to feel my heart beating and would try, by placing my hand on [my] chest, to feel if it wasn't stopping. It was undoubtedly in this way that I started counting to reassure myself. I counted very quickly between each beat and if I could succeed in passing a certain number before a particular beat, or in making the beats correspond with even or with uneven numbers, etc., I felt reassured. (1967, p. 136 ff)

Another relates:

> I often accompany my father when he goes to the rifle range. While my father shoots I sit on a bench. He gives me his cigar to hold. I imagine I can influence the accuracy of his shot by the position of the cigar. According as the cigar is almost vertical (the lighted end downwards), or at an angle of 90°, 120°, or 180°, the shot will be fairly good, good, or excellent. The shot never entirely misses since my father is a good shot. However,

after two or three good shots have been fired, I lower the cigar for a while, with the feeling that he cannot keep this up. (1967, p. 137)

Other magical actions of this sort can be found in the well-known children's practice of not walking on the lines of the pavement, or of touching every fencepost or every parking meter along their route. One of Piaget's collaborators notes:

When I particularly wanted something, I often used to step on every other stone as I walked on the pavement. If I succeeded in doing this as far as the end of the pavement it was a sign that what I wanted would happen. Or I would touch the stones of a wall, tapping every third stone and if I thus succeeded in reaching the last stone of the wall, I was certain of my success, etc. (1967, p. 138)

Similarly, Piaget notes that some actions having a specific origin, such as children's drawing their blankets over themselves to protect themselves from fears of the dark or strange sounds, eventually become dissociated from their original context and become rites, thus acquiring an intrinsic, magical value of their own:

[One collaborator] felt protected if on getting into bed the clothes were completely tucked in all round so that she could slip in without anywhere unmaking the bed. If by chance she found the clothes not tucked in, or that they had come unmade as she got in, she felt herself threatened by danger. (1967, p. 140)

Besides the belief in magic through actions and objects, the child believes in magic through participation between thought and things. Some of these magical beliefs consist simply of thinking of something to make a particular event happen or not, as in children's thinking the opposite from what they really want, "as if reality made a point of intentionally foiling [their] desires" (1967, p. 142). One manifestation of this sort of magic between thought and things is the child's use of various words or names to influence events. Piaget reports:

Seated a couple of feet away from his cat and staring into the cat's eyes, [a certain naturalist, as a child] would pronounce many times the formula: "Tin, tin, pin, pin de l'o-ü-in, pin, pin, tin, tin, pin, pin, de l'o-ü-in, pin, pin . . ., etc." So far as memory is to be trusted, the aim of this formula was to enable the child to project his personality into the cat: While pronouncing it the child felt himself pervading the cat's being and thus dominating it by participation. (1967, p. 141)

Clan first succumbed to masturbation at Mayens-de-Sion. When he came home, he tried under the sway of remorse not to suppress the memory but to suppress the fact itself. . . . To bring this about, it was against the actual name of Mayens-de-Sion that he set himself: "I did all I could to break the name of Mayens-de-Sion." To break the name, he simply distorted it. He repeated the name aloud, pronouncing it in German, *Máyenserséyens*, and accentuating the two syllables "may" and "sey." (1967, p. 141)

Though Piaget does not make the connection, it is easy to see how the use of thoughts and words to influence events is related closely to a final type of magical conviction, that is, belief in magical acts by commandment, where the will of one object can act of itself on that of others. Piaget observed that these participations are frequently connected with the idea of the obedience of objects:

[One of Piaget's friends] believed during many years of his childhood (though he had never before revealed it) that he was the "ruler" of the world, that is to say that he could make the sun, the moon, the stars, and the clouds move as he willed them. (1967, p. 146)

Magic and the tale. Turning to the fairy tale, one realizes that the magical relationships that exist in the child's conception of the world exist as well in the world of the tale, which, in fact, is a world suffused with magic. Just as objects, actions, thoughts, words, and will can exercise magical influence over events in the child's world, so can they be found to exercise similar influence in the world of the fairy tale. The magical influence of actions on events, for instance, pervades the fairy tale. In its purest form, it is this type of magic that accounts for the ability of the prince, through the action of kissing the enchanted princess in "Sleeping Beauty" (P)[2] or "Briar Rose" (G), to awaken her from her spell, and it accounts for the ability of the enchanted swans in "The Six Swans" (G), through the action of breathing on one another, to restore themselves to their human forms. More often, however, this type of magic by action appears in the tales in connection with a magical object; that is, the object is acted upon, or some action is performed with the object, and a magical occurrence re-

---

[2]Throughout this and the remaining chapters, the designations (P), (G), or (A) after the title of a fairy tale indicates the tale's author, respectively, Perrault, the Grimms, or Andersen.

sults. This combined function of magic by action and magic by object appears in stories such as "The Tinderbox" (A), where the tinderbox, upon being struck, produces the dogs which aid the soldier, and "The Blue Light" (G), where the soldier's lighting of his pipe with the blue light produces the tiny black man who brings the soldier's fortune. Similarly, in "The Knapsack, the Hat, and the Horn" (G), the son makes his way through the world, escaping danger and always triumphing through the aid which comes his way whenever he taps his knapsack, turns his hat, or blows his horn. And it is the actual throwing of the nettle shirts over the enchanted swans in "The Wild Swans" (A) that returns them to human form. Not infrequently, the action is connected with one object which resembles another. In "Cinderella" (P), for instance, the godmother changes the pumpkin into a gilded coach, the mice into grey horses, a large rat into a fat coachman, and the lizards into footmen. Operating on the basis of quantity are the transformations in "The Twelve Brothers" (G), where the maiden's picking of the twelve white lilies causes her brothers to become twelve enchanted black ravens.

The magical relationship between thought and things which exists in the child's world exists in the fairy tale world in the form of wishes. Characters need only wish for something to occur and their wishes are somehow fulfilled. In "Cinderella" (G), for instance, the long-suffering daughter has but to wish at the tree that grows upon her mother's grave and the white bird throws down to her whatever she wants. "The Pink" (G) proceeds in similar fashion: the young prince is endowed very early in his life with the power of wishing—whatever he wants will be granted to him. The influence of thoughts on events, however, does not always produce such salutary results, and many tales are built on the harm that can come from foolish wishes. In "The Seven Ravens" (G), the father who rashly wishes his tardy sons were turned into ravens soon gets his wish. The husband and wife in "The Ridiculous Wishes" (P) waste their first two wishes in petty quarreling, and then must use the third and last to undo the harm they have already done. Frequently the wishes of the fairy tale are expressed by means of an incantatory formula, and it is here that a magical thought in the form of a wish, in combination with words, can become a manifestation of magic by commandment. Only a few examples are necessary: The sons in "The Table, the Ass, and the Stick" (G) command the table by means of the formula "Table be covered"; the ass by "Bricklebrit"; and the stick by "Stick, out of the sack!" In "Sweet Porridge" (G), the words "Cook, little pot, cook" cause the porridge to come forth, but when the mother forgets the words "Stop, little pot, stop" the porridge flows over the whole town. And in the Grimms' "Cinderella," the young girl commands the birds to help her and uses the formula "The good into the pot,/The bad into the crop"; she then commands the hazel tree to dress her, saying "Shiver and quiver, my little tree,/Silver and gold throw down on me."

Words in the form of names figure importantly in some tales. In "Rumplestiltskin" (G), it is the discovery of the dwarf's name that enables the queen to gain power over him and release her child and herself from his demands. The young prince in "Iron Hans" (G) also can influence events with a name, and has but to say "Iron Hans," the name of a rust brown iron man, and Hans will come to help him.

Animist Beliefs in Child and Tale

Animism and the child. Piaget showed that magical beliefs of the child are integrally connected with belief in animism, where the child regards as living and conscious a large number of inanimate objects. Piaget (1967) distinguished four successive types and corresponding stages of animistic belief in the child (p. 169 ff). For children of the first stage, which lasts until ages 6 or 7, all objects may be conscious, even if stationary, but consciousness is connected with activity of some kind, whether this activity arises in the objects themselves or is imposed upon them from without. Thus, a stone may feel nothing until it is moved; a piece of wood may not be conscious but will feel its burning when set afire. In the second stage, which lasts from 6-7 to 8-9, the child assigns consciousness only to things that can move, those whose special function it is to be in motion. Thus, the sun and moon, rivers, carts, bicycles, watches are all regarded as conscious. In the third stage, which lasts from 8-9 to 11-12, the child makes an essential distinction between movement that is introduced by an outside agent, as can be the case in the first and second stages, and movement by the object itself. Consciousness is restricted to bodies that can move of themselves. Thus, fire, clouds, and water can feel things, but bicycles, cars, and trains cannot. In the fourth stage, which is not usually reached until 11-12, consciousness is restricted to animals. The concept of "thing" (lifeless object) becomes quite developed; consciousness is denied, for instance, to clouds, fire, or flowers, and is restricted to animals, people, and insects.

The degree of systematization of animist beliefs is, of course, much less than the above listing implies. Piaget maintained, and later research agreed, that animism is much more a general trend of mind than a consciously systematic belief, and with an individual child studied over a period of time animism is always varying. Even if this were not the case, and children did, in fact, progress from one Piagetian stage of animism to another in consistent fashion, the stages that include children between the ages of 6 and 8, the ages of peak interest in the fairy tale, are characterized by such diffuse and non-restrictive animism that none of the types of animism to be found in the fairy tale is excluded.

Animism and the tale. The type of animism having to do with objects which can be active—objects which move of themselves or can be set into motion—is found in "Sweetheart Roland" (G). Here a maiden lets fall, in various parts of the house, three drops of blood from her murdered sister's head, and later, in answer to the stepmother's question "Where art thou?" the three drops of blood speak with human voices and answer: "Here on the stairs," "Here in the kitchen warming myself," and "Here in bed, sleeping."

The type of animism having to do with objects whose special function it is to be in motion is found in "The Seven Ravens" (G). Here the conscience-stricken daughter, seeking the release of her brothers, travels to the end of the world. There she is rebuffed by the hot and terrible sun, which devours children, as well as by the dismal and dreary moon. The stars, however, befriend her. Sitting on their own special seats, one of them, the Morning Star, speaks and gives her a little bone which will open the mountain wherein lie her brothers.

The most common type of animism in the tale, however, is one which attributes consciousness to animals. A large number of these instances involve speaking animals who are actually humans who have been transformed. The frog in "The Frog Prince" (G) speaks, eats at the princess's table, sleeps in her bed, and finally, after being thrown against a wall, is released from his enchantment and becomes a prince again. The bear in "Snowwhite and Rose Red" (G), the lion in "The Lady and the Lion" (G), and many others are all of this sort. More strictly animist are those instances where the animal is distinguished not by the fact that it is an enchanted human, but by the fact that it can speak. It is because the servant overhears the ducks talking in "The White Snake" (G) that he is able to learn that one of them has swallowed the queen's ring. The doves in "Cinderella" (G) reveal the stepsisters' treachery by crying to the prince: "Prithee, look back, prithee look back/There's blood on the track/The shoe is too small/At home is the true bride waiting thy call." Other such animals are the cat in "Puss in Boots" (P), the flounder in "The Fisherman and His Wife" (G), and the wolf in "Little Red Riding Hood" (P), (G).

Morality in Child and Tale

The two moralities of the child. Correspondences exist between the moral system that children maintain in their world and the moral system that exists in the world of the fairy tale. In his *The Moral Judgment of the Child* (1965), Piaget develops a theory summarized by Flavell (1963). There appear to be two moralities in children, the earlier being a morality of constraint. It is formed in the context of unilateral relations between the child as inferior and the adult as superior. The child accepts the prohibitions and sanctions handed down from above and treats them as moral absolutes, unquestioned and sacred. Thus the child views wrong-doing in objective rather than subjective terms, is confined to the letter rather than the spirit of the law, and does not see actions either in terms of the inner motives of the actor or in terms of the social meaning of the act itself. Only overt consequences count in determining the wrongfulness of acts, not the inner intention and motives involved. Similarly, justice is simply whatever the authority commands rather than an equitable distribution of punishments and rewards meaningfully related to the acts which gave rise to them. As the child develops, this morality of constraint is replaced, but only partially, by a morality of co-operation formed out of the reciprocal relationships with other children and based on mutual rather than unilateral respect. With a growing understanding of the role of motives in their own and others' actions, children come to the basis of morality, and begin to view moral action as an autonomous good, essential to the functioning of any group of people. With this understanding, rules become rational rather than arbitrary, wrong-doing is judged by motivational as well as objective criteria, and justice is seen in terms of equality and equity.

It is the earlier of these two developmental periods, when the morality of constraint prevails, which encompasses the age level under present investigation. So it is appropriate to mount a detailed examination of that period, and in particular of the child's attendant attitude toward what is generally known as retributive and distributive justice.

Retributive justice and expiatory punishment in the child and the tale. During that period defined by a morality of constraint, the child's notion of retributive justice—that system whereby rewards and punishments are meted out for merit or guilt—is characterized by what Piaget (1965) calls the child's belief in expiatory punishment. With expiatory punishment there is no relation between the content of the guilty act and the nature of its punishment. The way of setting things right is to powerfully coerce individuals back to their duty and to bring home their guilt to them by means of a powerful punishment (p. 205). For the children Piaget examined, punishment consisted of inflicting upon the guilty a pain that would "smart enough" to make them realize the gravity of their misdeed. In response to certain stories of moral dilemmas, Piaget's subjects consistently thought that retributive justice was most just when it was most severe. "It is worse," said one in choosing a harsh punishment; "That will punish him most," said another (p. 213).

Such retributive justice through expiatory punishment abounds in the fairy tales, finding expression in the harsh fate that invariably befalls wrong-doers. The scoundrel cook in "The Pink" (G), for having deceived the king, is forced to eat live coals until flames pour out of his mouth and is eventually torn into four quarters. The maid-in-waiting in "The Goose Girl" (G), for having posed as the true princess, is put naked into a barrel stuck with nails and is dragged along by horses from street to street until she is dead. But such obviously expiatory punishments are by no means the only sort that exist in fairy tales. There are many instances of a close connection between the content of the guilty act and the nature of its punishment. In "King Thrushbeard" (G), the proud and haughty princess is appropriately humbled by being forced to be a beggar woman who must suffer all sorts of humiliation. The inordinate desire for wealth and position that possesses the wife in "The Fisherman and His Wife" (G) is punished by her being reduced to her original common existence. The sisters in "Cinderella" (G), concerned as they are with only the surface beauty of things, are stricken with blindness.

Now it would appear that these latter punishments, rather than corresponding to Piaget's notion of expiatory punishment, belong to another form of retributive justice—punishment by reciprocity, where the pain of punishment is not inflicted for its own sake, but rather to make the transgressor realize the nature of his misdeeds. Belief in punishment by reciprocity, however, does not occur in the earlier period of morality of constraint, but rather, in the later period of morality of co-operation. If this is the case, then an attempt to show correspondences between the morality of the young child and the morality of the fairy tale has seemingly met an insurmountable obstacle. But a moment's reflection will show that however appropriate it is from the viewpoint of reciprocity to have those who revel in sights lose their sight, a punishment which involves the gouging out of eyes is certainly expiatory. Thus though some of the most memorable punishments in fairy tales can be seen as reciprocity, they are also expiatory, and therefore do correspond to the young child's notion of just punishment.

Distributive justice and adult authority in the child and the tale. Piaget (1965) also discovered that during the morality-of-constraint period, characterized as it is by a retributive justice where expiatory punishment prevailed, the child's sense of distributive justice—that system whereby reward and punishment are divided among those of merit or guilt—is almost entirely dependent upon the notion that whatever is commanded by the adult is just. Respect for authority predominates, and though older children from ages 7-8 to 11-12 associate distributive justice with equality (where all must be treated equally, regardless of circumstances) and eventually with equity (where strict equality is overlooked in favor of extenuating circumstances) the 6 to 8 year-old does not consider motivation or circumstance in the distribution of justice because for him justice is whatever authority decrees (p. 263 ff).

This preoccupation with adult authority and lack of concern with motivation have interesting correspondences in the fairy tale. For the child, the laws of the world are the laws of the adult, and to violate the laws of the adult is to violate the laws of the world. Similarly, in the fairy tale, the laws of the world are located in the adult or authority figures—the old kings, the crones along the roadside, the fairy godmothers, the mysterious husbands, and the like. To transgress their rules is actually to transgress the entire world order. Thus for the wife in "Bluebeard" (P) to unlock the last and forbidden door is not merely an act of disobedience to her husband, but is as well a violation of that pervasive rule in the world of the fairy tale that insists that injunctions and other prohibitions be observed. The same is true of Snow White's (G) ignoring the warning of the seven dwarfs not to let anyone in the house. Similarly, the reluctant daughter in "The Frog Prince" (G), by not keeping her word, offends not only the king and the frog, but also that law, so often found in the fairy tale, which demands that what is promised must be performed.

In the face of such authority, it is small wonder that motivation and circumstances in the world of the fairy tale, as in the child's conception of the world, are negligible considerations. With the fairy tale as with the child, it is the deed rather than the motivation behind it that matters. Piaget's subjects (1965), when faced with the story of a boy who, mischievously playing with his father's ink pot, makes a little blot on the tablecloth, and the story of another boy who, wanting to help his father by filling the ink pot, makes a big blot on the tablecloth, judged as naughtier the child who made the big blot, evaluating the actions in terms of their material results rather than the intentions behind them (p. 122 ff).

So too in the fairy tale. It does not matter that it is because his wife is dying that the husband in "Rapunzel" (G) steals the lettuce from the witch's garden; the theft has angered the witch and the couple's first child must be forfeited. Similarly, the fact that there were not enough gold plates for all the fairies in the kingdom in "Sleeping Beauty" (P) or "Briar Rose" (G) does not lessen the insult to the slighted fairy, and the young princess thus receives not only gifts but a curse as well. It is the trickery of the princesses in "The Twelve Dancing Princesses" (G) that causes each suitor to fail in his attempt at discovering their evening escapades, but this does not alter the fact that the king's decree of death for all failures is to be fulfilled. And it is only because the sister in "The Twelve Brothers" (G) wishes to grace the table with flowers that she picks the lilies in the garden, but she has trespassed, and her brothers are thus changed into ravens and she is doomed to silence.

Causal Relationships in Child and Tale

The relationship between motivation and deed can also be viewed as the relationship between cause and effect, making relevant Piaget's studies of the child's notions of causality, reported in *The Language and Thought of the Child* (1955) and *Judgment and Reasoning in the Child* (1968).

Causality and the child. Piaget (1955, 1968) states that in children's retelling of stories and in their explanations of the workings of mechanical devices, causal relations are rarely expressed, but instead are generally indicated by a simple juxtaposition of related terms. The child lays stress on the events themselves rather than on the relations of time or cause which unite them, preferring factual description to causal explanation. The child's mode of expression consists of connecting propositions with "and then," which indicates neither a temporal, nor a causal, nor a logical relation, but rather a purely personal connection between ideas as they arise in the mind of the explainer.

Causality and the tale. In a word, this tendency in the child's thinking is paratactic, and it corresponds to the paratactic characteristic of the fairy tale (cf. Fischer 1963) where the tale's causal relations, however precisely controlled they may be, are not explicitly expressed. It is, of course, an overstatement to say that causal relations remain consistently inexplicit in the tale, but it is generally true that with the tale, as with the child, juxtaposition carries the burden of expressing causal relations. For example, the following passages from certain tales of the Grimms show that while "and" or "and then" serve to indicate at least temporal relations, the causal relations are much less near the surface of the narration.

> But he knew what to do, and spat out once or twice behind the carriage some of the sea-water which he had drunk, and a great lake arose in which the warriors were caught and drowned. (Stern, p. 606)

> They cut the apple of life in two and ate it together; and then her heart became full of love for him, and they lived in undisturbed happiness to a great age. (p. 101)

Egocentrism in Child and Tale

Though the above discussion of magic, animism, morality, and causality by no means exhausts either the characteristics of the fairy tale or the characteristics of the child, one additional dimension of both child and tale will be examined for the possibility of further correspondences.

Egocentrism and the child. Piaget's most generalized theory about children has to do with egocentrism, a concept which defies nominal definition, but which Piaget maintains is brought about by certain conditions of the child and his world. One group of conditions consists of those of an individual nature, that is, those bound up with the consciousness of children as it derives fro... their own activity. About such factors Piaget (1967) holds that in the child there is a lack of differentiation between consciousness of the action of self on the self, and consciousness of the action of self on things. The child's mind does not distinguish, or does so but dimly, the self from the external world, and thus the world is regarded as a continuous whole with equivalent feelings, desires, and the like. The other group of conditions consists of those of a social nature, that is, those bound up with the relations felt by children to exist between them and their environment, particularly between them and their parents. Piaget maintains that children see their parents, like the parts of their own bodies, as objects that can be moved in continual response to their desires; every cry of the child brings action on the part of the parents, and even the child's unexpressed desires are anticipated and fulfilled. The resultant egocentrism, of course, gradually gives way to socialization, but Piaget found (1967), and later studies agreed (cf. Flavell, p. 399 ff), that egocentrism is tenacious indeed. Even during the years under present investigation, there is considerable continuity between the children's activities and those of their parents; the children still live with the impression that their thoughts, aims, and desires are known and shared by those around them.

Egocentrism and the tale. Turning to the fairy tale, one realizes that the relationship of the hero to his world is much the same as the relationship of children to theirs. Just as the children are situated at the center of a universe, the forces of which seemingly operate on their behalf, so the hero of the fairy tale exists at the center of his world, the events of which, however initially adverse, consistently conjoin in myriad ways to enable him to fulfill his desires. Perrault's Cinderella is delivered from adversity through her godmother's transforming of the rags, pumpkin, and mice into magnificent robes, coach, and horses. In the Grimms' version all the benign forces in the world come together in the hazel tree which showers down fine garments upon Cinderella, thus enabling her beauty, overlooked until now because of her lowly position, to be magnificently displayed and deservedly seen by the prince. In "The Golden Bird" (G), the prince's great task is to find the golden horse, and though he fails on many occasions to heed the warnings of the fox, the fox forgives him each time and continually protects him from danger. Though the hedge that surrounds the sleeping princess in both "Briar Rose" (G) and "Sleeping Beauty" (P) foils all others who approach, it parts for the handsome prince so that he alone might reach the lovely girl. Nowhere in the tales is the existence of a hero-serving world more clearly seen than in this passage from the Grimms' version:

> When the prince approached the briar hedge, it was in blossom, and was covered with beautiful large flowers which made way for him of their own accord and let him pass unharmed, and then closed up again into a hedge behind him. (Stern, p. 240)

The comparisons here of the characteristics of the child and the characteristics of the fairy tale permit a fairly clear observation: just as magic and animism suffuse the world of the fairy tale, so do they suffuse the world of the child; just as a morality of constraint prevails in the fairy tale, so does it prevail in the moral system of the child; just as the fairy tale world and its hero become one in achieving his ends, so do children believe their world is one with them; and just as causal relations remain unexpressed in the fairy tale, so do they remain unexpressed in the child's communication. Other characteristics of the child's mind and the tale's construction surely exist, but those examined here warrant the conclusion that precise correspondences between child and tale do indeed exist. In a very real sense the tale embodies an accurate representation of the child's conception of the world.

CHAPTER FOUR

ESTABLISHING AN EXPLANATION FOR CHILDREN'S INTEREST IN FAIRY TALES

The question, "What is it about both children and fairy tales, when they come together at some times and not others, that causes interest to occur?" requires, with the words, "when they come together . . . ," description of how the characteristics of reader and tale interact to produce interest. Thus, while the previous chapter has shown that correspondences exist between the child's mind and the tale's construction, that does not in itself explain the interest phenomenon. Such an explanation will come about only through determining how this correspondence of characteristics actually functions in producing the interest phenomenon.

Many other explanations have been offered at one point or another, and it will be useful first to examine some of the major ones.

Anthropological Explanations

Of the many possible ways of viewing the fairy tale, one is to see it as having an actual basis in fact, encapsulating and stabilizing certain customs and practices of an earlier age. It might be, for instance, that the persistent theme of the youngest son or daughter who overcomes the treachery or jealousy of elder brothers and sisters and thereby achieves success has its origins, as Macculloch (1905) maintains, in those laws of inheritance known as *Jungstenrecht*, which were at one time more prevalent than primogeniture, establishing the *youngest* child as the principal heir (p. 351 ff). Similarly, the recurrent theme of prohibition, where dire circumstances attend the violation of a particular interdiction, has its origins in the fact that among primitive peoples the sacred grove, the fetish halls, and all such places were not to be rashly approached, since the owner of a fetish incurred danger or loss of power if someone intruded (p. 306 ff).[1]

---

[1] A further discussion of the origins of the youngest child and the prohibition themes will be found in Appendix C.

As is clear from the above, one cannot long continue taking note of past customs and practices embedded in the tales without also taking into account the construction of the mind that lay behind them. The tale may not only stabilize certain objective occurrences of the past, but may also stabilize a particular, earlier state of consciousness. In his monumental compilation of the attributes of the primitive mentality, for instance, Werner (1948) describes the primitive mind as being characterized by diffuseness, wherein the totality of a phenomenon overrules its differentiation into elements, and by syncretism, wherein there is no fundamental difference between subjective phenomena and objective phenomena—all of which results in a fusion of the inner world of ideas and personal strivings and the outer world of events (p. 339 ff). It is this mental configuration, Werner would say, which influences the way a primitive mentality construes the relationships between objects, events, words, and will. Also this set of mind gives rise to the myriad magical beliefs that characterize earlier states of consciousness.

Such a mentality is reflected in the fairy tale. An examination of the tale shows that its magical order may indeed be a vestige of a primitive magical perception of the world. For example, modern literary fantasies, which are products of more developed mentalities, have a magical order that causes magical objects and events to be met with a great deal of surprise and wonder by the characters. As Master Cherry, in Carlo Collodi's *The Adventures of Pinocchio*,[2] removes the bark from the log that is eventually to become Gepetto's puppet, he believes that he hears a voice, but finding no one around, continues with his ax:

> And taking up the ax he struck a tremendous blow on the piece of wood.
> "Oh! oh! You have hurt me!" cried the same little voice dolefully.
> This time Master Cherry was petrified. His eyes started out of his head with fright, his mouth remained open, and his tongue hung out almost to the end of his chin, like a mask on a fountain. As soon as he had recovered the use of his speech, he began to say, stuttering and trembling with fear:
> "But where on earth can that little voice have come from that said Oh! Oh!? Here there is certainly no living soul. Is it possible that this piece of wood can have learnt to cry and to lament like a child? I cannot believe it. This piece of wood,

---

[2]The edition used is: M. A. Murray, trans., *Carlo Collodi: The Adventures of Pinocchio* (New York: Airmont Publishing, 1966).

> here it is; a log for fuel like all the others, and thrown on the
> fire it would about suffice to boil a saucepan of beans . . . .
> How then?" (Murray, pp. 14-15)

In the fairy tale, on the other hand, these same sorts of objects
and events—magical wands and tables, talking beasts, swift trans-
locations, and instant transformations—occasion no wonder and
exist on quite the same footing as every other object or event.
Though the princess in "The Frog Prince" (G) drops her golden
ball into the well and begins to weep bitterly, she meets the next
event with more equanimity:

> And as she thus lamented, someone said to her: "What ails
> you, King's daughter? You weep so that even a stone would
> show pity."
> She looked round to the side from whence the voice came,
> and saw a frog stretching back and forth its big, ugly head from
> the water. "Ah, old water-splasher, is it you?" said she; "I am
> weeping for my golden ball, which has fallen into the well."
> (Stern 1944, p. 17 ff.)

The reason for the difference between these two magical orders
seems to be quite simply that the one which suffuses the tale—not
the one in the literary fantasy—is much more a remnant of the
same magical order that suffused the primitive's perception of the
world. Werner showed, for instance, that to the primitive there is
nothing mysterious, transcendental, or "mystical" about magic.
For the primitive, there is no complete differentiation between
magical and natural events; the basic tendencies of magical behavior proceed out of a kind of thinking which is quite intelligible, and has no mysterious import to the primitive himself. "Only
in higher civilizations," said Werner, "where natural and supernatural events are completely separated and where magic does not
pervade the whole culture, is it possible for the specifically mystic
experience to develop" (p. 352).

Through the kind of exploration demonstrated above, further instances of the primitive's conception of the world can be found in
the tale. For example, the paratactic narration of the fairy tale, described in the previous chapter, can be seen as a vestige of that
primitive inability to divide natural phenomena into two series—
causal conditions and the results of those conditions—and to think
of causes not as necessary conditions but as inseparable parts of a
continuous action (cf. Shumaker 1966, p. 61; Werner p. 306). As
Werner carefully demonstrated by his comparative method and as
can be gathered by reference to Chapter 3, such instances point to

a similarity between the mind of the primitive and the mind of a
child. Given this similarity, it is then but a small step to the explanation that children's interest in the tale occurs because their conception of the world and the conception of the world reflected in
the tale—the primitive's conception—are the same.

This is an attractive explanation which in one form or another
has many adherents. Hazard (1947) maintains that the child's interest in the tale occurs because every child repeats, through the
reading of the tales, the history of the race (p. 161). Cass (1967)
holds, more specifically, that part of the child's interest arises because the development of a moral code in the child recapitulates
the long-term development of those moral codes in mankind
which are found in the tales (p. 34). Closer inspection of this explanation, however, will show that there is much about it that requires it to be rejected.

The most obvious objection against an explanation based on the
similarities between the child's mind and the primitive's mind is
that it leads to currently unfashionable recapitulation theories.
This objection, however, is specious: to demonstrate the similarity
between the child's mind and the primitive's mind, or to utilize
this observation as is done in this explanation, is not to affirm the
notion of recapitulation at all. Much more to the point is that link-
ing the child's mentality with the primitive's in an attempt to account for the child's interest in the tale may actually be unneces-
sary. To say that the child turns to the tale because the tale reflects
a primitive mentality which can be shown to be the same as the
child's mentality is actually to say that children turn to the tale
because it reflects their own mentality. And that conclusion could
be reached solely by comparing the characteristics of the child
and the tale, as was done in the previous chapter, without any
reference to the primitive mind.

But even if one chose to approach the child's interest through
the primitive's interest, it is not sufficient to say that children turn
to the tale because it reflects their own, primitive-like conception
of the world. Such a statement does not account for why children,
or the primitive, would seek such a reflection of their world in the
first place. Thus an explanation of the child's interest based only
on the correspondences that exist among child, primitive, and tale,
or between child and tale—and which then posits that such interest obtains because of these correspondences—quite begs the
question. When Hadas (1962) states that the fairy tale's magic is
"attuned to the child's own view that the world is magical" (p. 12),
or when Frank (1941) states that to the child all the occurrences in

the fairy tales are "quite within the range of the possible" (p. 45), it must be recognized that, though the observations are accurate, they do not actually account for children's interest in the fairy tales. Again, they do not explain why children would want to seek reflection of their own world in the tale in the first place. The anthropological explanation is therefore inadequate, and the search for the reasons for the child's interest in the tales must continue elsewhere.

Jungian Explanations

Folklore studies have always had difficulty in explaining the wide-spread occurrence of the same motifs in many different tales. Those who subscribe to various monogenesis-diffusion theories would say that a particular motif arose in one place and gradually spread to other places; those who subscribe to theories of polygenesis would say that the several motifs arose in many different places quite independent of one another (cf. Dundes 1965, p. 53 ff). The former theories are in greater favor today, but the polygenesis theories continue to claim attention because, by assuming the psychic unity of man, they can explain a migrating tale's appeal to many different sorts of cultures, something which the monogenesis theories cannot do.

The assumption about man's psychic unity, of course, has always been questioned, but Jung, for one, maintained it and made it one of the central ideas of his work. He noted (1968b) that certain mythical elements could be observed among individuals for whom all knowledge of this kind was out of the question, and where indirect derivation from popular figures of speech or religious ideas that might have been known to them was impossible (1968b, p. 154). He concluded that these motifs, these primordial images—or archetypes, as he called them—were autochthonous revivals, quite independent of tradition. Further, he claimed they were inherent structural elements present not just in the unconscious psyche of the individual but of all men, and were part of that inherited, collective, psychic substratum which he called the collective unconscious (1968b, p. 155). Jung (1968a) also maintained that the objectified existence of many of these archetypes, including the one he called the archetype of the spirit, was to be found in various myths and fairy tales. He discovered that in the dreams of many of his patients, where insight, understanding, good advice, determination, planning, and the like were needed but could not be provided by the dreamer, there would appear in a dream an old man or animal who would in some way compensate for the dreamer's own state of spiritual deficiency (p. 207).

Jung traced the precise workings of this archetype of the spirit as it exists in the fairy tale. The old man, or the old crone, the talking animal, or other donor always appears when the hero is in a hopeless and desperate situation, one from which only profound reflection, a stroke of luck, or a spiritual function can extricate him. But because his own inadequacy prevents the hero from accomplishing this himself, the compensatory knowledge comes in the form of a personified thought, that is, in the shape of a sagacious and helpful old man. Invariably, the old man puts the hero to a moral test or asks questions such as Who? Why? Whence? Whither? for inducing self-reflection, for gathering together the assets of the whole personality at a critical moment when all the hero's spiritual and physical forces are challenged and need to be concentrated in order to "fling open the door of the future" (p. 219). The old man becomes, in effect, the means whereby the hero may mobilize his moral forces, and bring about that concentration of powers which brings assurance—always one of the best guarantees of success; the giving of the talisman or magical device, which invariably results from the questioning, then becomes the physical manifestation of the hero's coming upon the unexpected and improbable power to succeed.

It is hard to deny that such archetypes exist in man's unconscious and that coming upon them in objectified form in the fairy tale can evoke them for reader's awareness. Even a limited acquaintance with Bodkin's profound readings (1934) leaves one convinced that there are indeed motifs in all literature, and not the least in fairy tales, that can excite what Murray (1966) referred to as long slumbering, yet eternally familiar and fundamental human emotions (p. 2).

The question that remains is whether the type of Jungian response described above, applying as it does to the general reader, applies as well to the child—a question whose answer ultimately depends on whether such archetypes reside in the child at all. Substantial evidence about the existence of archetypes in the child has never been available. Recently, however, with the first publication of some little known essays of Jung on this very subject, it appears that the child's psyche is very far from being empty (1954b, p. 44) and that the dreams of three- and four-year-old children are strikingly mythological (1954a, p. 54), containing archetypes which are the cause of their decidedly adult character (cf. Fordham 1944, 1957). But this knowledge, at last grasped, brings the question no further toward resolution. If archetypes exist in humans from their very earliest years onward and if reading of fairy tales does in fact liberate these archetypes, then one would assume that the activating of the archetypes, and the resultant interest in the tales, would commence in the earliest years and would continue throughout a reader's life in a stable and consistent pattern. But as the research into children's reading interests has previously shown, this is not the case because after a period of intense interest in the tale, the child turns from it in contempt. The longitudinal pattern of children's reading interests then seems to be incompatible with the longitudinal pattern of the functioning of archetypes.

Now it may be that different archetypes predominate in the individual at different periods of development, that children are interested in the tale only as long as their own archetypes and the objectification of these archetypes in the tale correspond to one another. It may be that once their archetypes change, their interest in the tale, the archetypes of which do not change, wanes. Or, it may be that, with age, the grip of the archetypes upon the unconscious loosens, or becomes more deeply submerged, less responsive to the objectification that is found in the tales. All of these notions, however, depend upon a greater knowledge of archetypes and the collective unconscious than presently exists. They are so conjectural that a Jungian explanation of children's interest in the fairy tale, despite its attractiveness from an intuitive standpoint, is unacceptable.

Freudian Explanations

Another major explanation of children's interest in fairy tales grows out of Freudian psychology. Freud specifically excluded fairy tales from consideration in his own psychoanalytic work, perhaps because, as Bloom (1976) suggests, as stories where everything was possible and nothing was incredible, they did not provide him better clues than dreams and mistakes for the study of psychic conflicts. Perhaps it was because by ignoring the tales himself Freud could denigrate Jung's full excursion into them. But Freud's followers did not exclude fairy tales from their consideration, and so a large tradition of so-called Freudian interpretation has grown up around the tales. Hoffer (1931) maintains, for example, that the child's unconscious may correspond with the unconscious gist of the fairy tale. Briehl (1937) has shown how each detail in the development of the oedipus complex finds expression in one or another fairy tale theme. Friedlaender (1942) shows how the unconscious content of the fairy tale, tallying with the conflicts pertaining to the child's age, offers solutions and alleviates anxiety in the child. And Bettelheim (1976) has explained how the figures and events of fairy tales personfy inner conflicts and suggest to the child's unconscious how these conflicts may be solved and what the next steps toward a "higher humanity" (p. 26) might be.

There are a number of intelligent interpretations based on Freudian thinking. In an analysis of "The Three Golden Hairs," for example, Róheim (1922) shows how the giant is a father duplicate, transformed by the oedipal state of the boy in the tale. He further maintains the the pulling out of the giant's three golden hairs, which, as with Samson, are symbols of potency and thus the male organ, has its origins in the oedipus complex: the boy loves his mother, is jealous of his father, and wishes to punish him by castration for doing what he cannot do. With such interpretation, this story would thus embody for its hypothetical reader an opportunity to identify with its hero in terms of the difficulties that stand between him and a sexual object, and to deny the old-young dichotomy between boy and grown man which precludes the child's achieving the oedipal gratifications he seeks.

In an interpretation of the frog prince type of tale, where the frog, through repeated pleadings, is gradually admitted to increasing intimacy with the maiden and is finally released from the spell, Jones (1965) maintains that if in the unconscious the frog is a constant symbol of the male organ when viewed with disgust, then it is possible to say that the story represents the maiden's gradual overcoming of her aversion to it. The story would thus embody for the hypothetical reader a common instinctual situation, and would offer a means of reducing an unconscious anxiety.

Bettelheim's interpretations, more comprehensive than any to date, are in the same vein. In "Sleeping Beauty" (P) or "Briar Rose" (G), for example, the staircase the girl ascends stands for sexual experiences, the small door and the key in its lock stand for the female sexual organs, and the turning of the key in the lock, intercourse. The distaff which the old woman uses in spinning is the male organ, and when the girl touches it, she injures her finger and falls into a deep sleep, all of which would then be a warning to both child and parents of the destructive force of sexual arousal before mind and body are ready for it. Similarly, in "Hansel and Gretel" (G) the destruction that nearly befalls the two children when they blissfully eat away at the gingerbread house (the nourishing body of their original mothers) would show children the necessity of overcoming and sublimating their infantile orality and its associated parent dependencies.

Roheim, Jones, Bettelheim, and others have rendered these interpretations carefully. Yet at least two irresolvable problems exist. The first problem is a general one, having to do with approaching texts through symbolic interpretations. Such an approach is predicated on the notion that behind a story's manifest text of observable events and characters is a latent text of hidden meanings and symbols and that the reader responds to the features of the latent text rather than to the features of the manifest text. This approach thus interprets the manifest content of a story in order to expose its latent content of symbols, and then posits the way the reader responds to these symbols as externalizations of the internal processes of his psyche. The problem here is that this approach ignores the fact that the reader knows only the author's manifest text and not the interpreter's reconstruction of it; thus all statements about the reader's response to the latent text refer to a conjunction of reader and text which never occurred. In a world where even the very notion of a normative, general reader is suspect, there is quite enough improbability about the nature of the reader's response to the manifest text. But the attempt to construct an hypothesis about the nature of the reader's response to a latent text—itself an hypothetical construction—becomes even more questionable.[3]

The latent meanings which the Freudian interpretations suggest are imbedded in the manifest content of the fairy tales may indeed be there. And a child may respond to these latent meanings in the ways these interpretations suggest. But even so, there can be no assurance that the latent meanings being responded to, in spite of the possible universality of symbols, are the ones hypothecated by the interpreter. In short, though much the same could be said about all explanations of reading interest, those explanations which rely on symbolic interpretations are *sui generis* explanations, and so more than any other kind of explanation, cannot use-

---

[3]For this reason Bettelheim's *The Uses of Enchantment* (1976), which proceeds primarily by means of symbolic interpretations, must be read less with delight than consternation. Even though he has written a work unequaled in its comprehensiveness, his interpretations in effect create a whole new reservoir of stories unread by any reader, let alone any child. Also, it is understandable that Bettelheim should inveigh against regression and denial, since all of his work with autistic children has probably led him to deplore any kind of retreat and to value most highly the immediate and active engagement with the world, an engagement that is so lacking in the children to whom he has devoted himself.

fully or even rightfully be extended from interpreter to reader or from reader to reader.

The second problem is a more specific one, having to do with the general orientation of the Freudian interpretations. The Freudian explanation of the child's interest in fairy tales rests entirely on the notion of infantile sexuality. Even though the single-mindedness of this orientation has a certain elegance and consistency, it is so completely reductive that it draws everything in the child's make-up into the orbit of sexual interpretation, with the result that the concept of sexuality is given unrealistic proportions. Although hardly the most temperate of Freudian critics, Jung (1954c) summarized at the outset what has been increasingly accepted, namely, that even though a child may be preoccupied with matters which for adults have an undoubtedly sexual cast, this does not prove that the nature of the child's preoccupation is to be regarded as equally sexual. Thus the "polyvalent" disposition of the child should not be documented with the sexual terminology borrowed from the stage of full-fledged sexuality (p. 7).

And so, though it is by no means the intent here to deny symbolic interpretations or that infantile sexuality influences the child's response to the tales, the Freudian explanation is too reductive by virtue of its emphasis on infantile sexuality, and too symbolic by virtue of its emphasis on latent content.[4]

The Present Explanation

In Chapter 3 it was easy to speak of this or that Piagetian characteristic of child thought, or of the child's conception of the world. But in focusing on these characteristics, one could miss seeing that, in relation to the whole continuum of an individual's mental development, these characteristics do not last long, being rapidly supplanted by other characteristics. Indeed, the very notion of Piagetian stages requires that children's thinking be seen not only in terms of its characteristics at any moment, but also in terms of the changes these characteristics undergo at every moment.

The point is crucial. It is true that children's conception of the world is characterized by egocentrism, animism, magic, morality of constraint, and the like. It is equally true that children's contact with each other, the intractableness of objects and persons to their will, the decreasing service of their parents—in short, all those

---

[4]A further discussion of the problems of symbolic interpretation and infantile sexuality is found in Bettelheim's *The Uses of Enchantment* (1976).

experiences that move children from an egocentric to a socialized sphere—daily challenge their conception of the world, altering that conception so that it becomes more compatible with the real world and causing them to abandon an earlier version. Experience causes children to be *dis*-illusioned and their state to be characterized by crisis. It is just such a crisis of experience which occurred when, as a result of hearing his father say something that was not quite true, Gosse (1908) found that not all knowledge resided in his parents:

> Here was the appalling discovery, never suspected before, that my father was not as God, and did not know everything. The shock was not caused by any suspicion that he was not telling the truth . . . but by the awful proof that he was not, as I had supposed, omniscient. (p. 36)

Piaget (1967) was aware of these crisis points, and noted, in addition, that it is usually just when implicit convictions are about to be shattered that they are for the first time consciously affirmed and most tenaciously held (p. 191). Another way of viewing this phenomenon is through the concept of regression, which maintains that, when an individual must make some difficult adjustment in his thinking or behavior, he is likely to revert to a less mature response (cf. Freud 1950b; Kris, 1944).[5] But if a romantic world dies for a child, it lives on in the fairy tale. With its construction of animism, magic, morality of constraint, and its whole egocentric cast, the fairy tale retains in stable form, impervious to change, the very conception of the world the child now finds challenged. In the face of that challenge, with the resultant crisis and regressive impulse, the child under 8 must turn to the fairy tale for a reaffirmation of his original conception of the world—a world preserved in the tale, unchanged and unchallenged.

Support for this hypothesis can be found in some of Lesser's observations (1957) about the reader of fiction. Lesser notes that at no stage of their lives do humans enjoy unbroken happiness, free of strivings, frustrations, or complexities; instead, humans encounter various anxieties and discontents, dissatisfactions and disillusionments that seem to be inevitable aspects of their experience (p. 20). Some persons attempt to minimize the significance of these painful occurrences by treating them as exceptional or accidental; or with eternal hope, but those who are honest with them-

---

[5]A further discussion of the concept of regression, will be found in Bettelheim's *The Uses of Enchantment*.

selves face the possibility that there may be something about life itself which is inimical to mankind's desire for perfect happiness (p. 20). At the same time, maintains Lesser, whatever else humans may be, they are indefatigable seekers of pleasure. If human experience does not yield enough satisfaction, they strive to reduce the discontent and augment the meager satisfactions it does offer by creating other, more harmonious worlds, worlds which accommodate their desires and to which they can repair, however briefly, for refuge, solace, and pleasure (p. 21). These other worlds, Lesser points out, exist in fiction, to which humans can turn to remedy the deficiencies of experience; the reading of fiction can "transport the reader to a realm more comprehensible and coherent, more passionate and more plastic, and at the same time more compatible with his ideals" (p. 39).

The relationships between Lesser's observations and the present hypothesis are manifest. Children's conception of a world where they believe they are one in consciousness with everything else, where thinking seemingly makes things so, where moral action is comfortably delineated by outer authority, where all forces seem to serve their egocentric ends is a conception that gradually changes. Through the process of socialization, children learn a different world, one where they are not in communion with all that is around them, where morality of action is hammered out in interaction with others, where all the world's forces do not, in fact, serve their ends. The child's conception of the world is thus a shifting one. Given the perplexity that surely results from such a situation, as well as the adaptations and adjustments that it requires, the child is undoubtedly characterized by the stresses that Lesser ascribes to the general reader. Undoubtedly also, children seek relaxation of these tensions, redress of these imbalances, safe haven from the disruption caused by the crisis of experience, and, in the manner of Lesser's general reader, seek a fictive world. In the world of the fairy tale, the world order that they once knew continues in stable form, and they may achieve again the satisfaction of experiencing a world that functions in accord with their desires.

Response to content. The experiencing of a fictional world is more specifically described by Wolf and Fiske's classic study (1949) of children's interest in comic books. There it is shown that, as children come to realize that the world is a very large and confusing place over which they have little control, they can, through the mechanism of denial,[6] remove themselves and enter the world of the story where, through identification with the hero,[7] they can be reassured of their power. Identifying with the comic book hero and his inevitable triumph and comforted by the unvarying portrayals of good people being rewarded and bad people being punished, children are temporarily set at ease in their own world, which, they are beginning to see, does not actually function with such personal satisfaction or structural simplicity. Evidently, the mechanisms of denial and identification that operate in children's reading of comic books also account for their absorption with the fairy tale. Just as magic, animism, and morality of constraint characterize the world order of the fairy tale, so do they characterize the real world order as the child has believed it to be. In the world of the tale, however, these characteristics remain stable and constant, whereas in the world of the child, they are waning. At the same time, just as certain forces frustrate the hero of the fairy tale and others align themselves in his behalf, so move the forces of the world that children physically inhabit, thwarting their wishes and foiling their actions in some instances and supporting their intentions in others. For the hero in the tale, however, but not necessarily for the child in life, all forces ultimately conjoin in the most salutary ways so that all endeavors reach a successful completion. It is not difficult to see, therefore, how by denying the order of the real world and embracing the order of the world of the tale, children can consistently and at will have the pleasure of experiencing a world order with which they are comfortable and familiar. By identifying with the hero of the tale, they can vicariously achieve their ends, a pleasure which in life they are discovering occurs only erratically.

Response to form. Children's response to the world order and to the hero of the fairy tale, which can be seen as a response to the content of the tale, is probably complemented by their response to

---

[6]Denial can be defined as the use an individual makes of fantasy to defend himself against intolerable situations in external reality (cf. Cameron 1963, p. 370). Denial is a common source of reassurance against anxiety, helplessness, or a sense of inadequacy (cf. Cameron, p. 230; Freud 1952, p. 78 ff.).

[7]Identification is modeled after imitation, and its aims are to enable the individual to be like the other person, to be in some respect the same, to take the other's role and perform his functions. Importantly, identification contributes to the enrichment of the energies at the disposal of the ego and thus strengthens it (cf. Cameron, p. 175).

the *form* of the tale, and in particular to its unusually regulated patterns, a characteristic that even the occasional reader of the tale soon discovers. As was evidenced by the earlier analysis of the structure of the stories in the present reservoir, there are patterned contrastive repetitions throughout the fairy tale. The children in "Hansel and Gretel" (G) are abandoned in the woods on the first occasion, and after their safe return are left there again. The queen in "Snow White" (G), having failed initially to kill her step-daughter, goes to the dwarf's house on successive occasions, each time under a different guise and with a different ploy, to bring an end to the girl, while each attempt is followed by a repetition of the queen's questioning of her mirror. The first of the sisters in "Cinderella" (G) attempts to fit into the slipper and fails; the second attempts the same and fails; Cinderella attempts and succeeds.

Now it can be seen that these patterned contrastive repetitions have the effect of filling out the body of the narrative, at the same time prolonging tension and postponing its relaxation, which upon final resolution makes for an enhanced pleasure. But such patterned presentations may have other effects as well. In his explorations of the effects of fictive form on the general reader, Lesser speaks of the control that fiction manifests—its tendency to organize its material in patterned form—and speculates that the mastery of material implied in this pattern suggests both the reassuring limits that parents place upon children's existence as well as the powers that children attribute to their parents. The degree of the reader's absorption, his naive delight in the skill of the storyteller, his unquestioning acceptance of the values which inhere in a particular story—all these seem to suggest a relation to a parental figure (p. 126 ff). If this is the case with adult readers, who no longer need the reassuring aspects of parental control, it must be much more the case for children at the stage of development under present investigation, children who may be seeking to retain whatever they can of their once unshakable convictions about their parents' power. Children—now no longer confident in their parents' knowledge or power, no longer experiencing either the reassuring control exercised upon the world in their behalf or the unerring validity of the stringencies placed upon them—must find in the controlled form of the fairy tale an opportunity to experience that original pleasure of assurance they once had in life.

Other aspects of form merit consideration. Patterned contrastive repetition can be seen as a manifestation of the tale's overriding tendency to be symmetrical, a characteristic to which, as Olrik

(1965) points out in his formulation of the laws of folk narrative, all characters and events are invariably subordinated. In addition to this symmetry of structure within the individual tale, however, there is the symmetry of structure that exists between all tales, giving the impression that the stories are all of a kind. The earlier references to Propp's scheme (1968), for instance, showed that, though individual characters or specific details may change from tale to tale, basic actions and types of characters do not. It was also demonstrated that the basic actions and the types of characters are so similar in all tales that, even when the relationships between these actions and types of characters exhibit wide divergence from the majority of tales, as they do in stories such as those of Andersen, these differences become obscured and for the most part go unnoticed. At the same time, attributes of the characters and events in the tales ignore the formal boundaries of individual tales and attach themselves freely to the characters and events in all the tales. Thus, though only some wells in the tales are enchanted, this attribute is shared by all wells in whatever tale, and therefore all wells, if not enchanted at least possess the possibility of being so. For all characters there is the possibility that some misstep on their part will result in physical transformation, and all crones along the roadside, whether they demonstrate the fact or not, possess magical powers. The result of these similarities of structure and the transference of attributes is that it does not take children long to learn that having had the kind of experience they had with one tale, they can have it again with any tale. The reassurance is there from tale to tale, as it is not necessarily from one art story to another.

The length of the tale has its effects also. Because the tales are easily started and finished in a short period of time, the child is able to achieve gratification quickly within an individual tale. And by reading one tale after another, he is able to achieve it over and over again. This point is illumined by Olrik's observation that the tale begins by moving from calm to excitement and, after the hero's success, from excitement to calm (p. 132). Tension is increased and is felt as anxiety—just as was found with patterned contrastive repetition—and then is alleviated through an orderly and balanced conclusion. The success of the hero, because it invariably involves the conjoining of the forces in the fairy tale world to aid him in achieving his ends, is in effect a reaffirmation of children's belief in the egocentric cast of their own world. The terminal calm that follows satisfies children's desire for the security of the stable world they once knew. Seen in this light, the consolation of the happy ending that Tolkien (1964) speaks of takes on an added meaning; though such consolation certainly is to be found in other types of literature, it can nowhere else be experienced so swiftly and successfully.[8]

The above discussion of the relationship between the child and the content and form of the fairy tale should not obscure the point, however, that a tale's appeal to the child does not lie merely in the fact that it is suffused with animism and magic, that it is single-minded in its attention to its hero, that its morality is based upon the rule of authority, that it is characterized by regulated patterns, and so on. Indeed, one or another of these factors might be found in other literature available to children. Rather, the appeal is that only in the fairy tale do all these factors come together in unique conjunction and form an ambiance that children once believed characterized their own world. Wolf and Fiske (p. 13), as well as Peller (1959, p. 423) in another context, show how the child enjoys the gratification of a milieu not otherwise obtainable in reality. It is easy to see how children, in search through various mechanisms of another world more satisfying than their own, would find in the fairy tale the very world they seek.

Older Children, Adults, and the Fairy Tale

Older children. Children's pleasure is short-lived. As the research in reading interests has shown, the child's peak interest in fairy tales lasts only between the approximate ages of 6 and 8; after this age, there is a sharp decline in the child's interest in this type of story. This post-fairy tale age is not within the province of the present investigation, but it will be instructive to consider some possible causes of the dramatic decline in the child's interest in the tale.

The crisis of experience described above, which has been shown to cause the child to turn to the tale for stability and for a harkening back to a more comfortable existence, is not interminable. Every disillusioning experience at the same time instructs children as to what the world really is because each experience makes them more familiar with the configuration of the new world they are discovering. Steadily, their confidence in their grasp of

---

[8]That the story's ending plays a large part in the child's interest is further confirmed by Wolf and Fiske (p. 30) who observed that with comic books, children considered the story to be an irritating delay before the hero's final triumph over evil.

this new world, their assuredness of their position, reaches the point where they are comfortable enough in the real world to desire no longer a return to the old. When this point is reached, children no longer turn to the tale as a stay against change, but instead reject it as being too unlike the world they now know and to which they have become increasingly acclimated. The crisis of experience, which in the beginning causes children to cast backward glances, now causes them to look ahead. So the very tales which once provided a respite from the turmoil of that crisis now impede the forward glance; consequently, older children treat fairy tales with scorn and contempt.[9]

Children come to view the tales as improbable, indeed, impossible. While on the one hand they begin to turn away from them, on the other they seek stories which will stand the test of veracity, stories which can be loosely referred to as stories of reality. What influences the child's interest in these non-fairy tale books, however, may not necessarily be that they are representations of the world as it really is. Friedlaender (p. 136) argues convincingly that it is rather that these books gratify the child's desires after age 8, just as the fairy tale satisfied the child's earlier desires. For example, at this later stage of development, children's desire for separation from their parents, brought about perhaps by earlier disillusionment as to their parents' infallibility, becomes quite intense; that desire can find response in the separation themes that figures so prominently in stories such as *Heidi, Little Lord Fauntleroy, The Secret Garden*, and *A Little Princess*. Friedlaender's hypothesis seems reasonable. It is probable that, though particular desires may change from one stage of development to another, children's turning to the stories of reality, once they have discovered what reality is, is as much a function of seeking gratification, through the mechanisms of identification and denial, as was their turning to the fairy tale when they thought that what it represented was indeed reality—or more accurately, what they wanted reality to be.

Adults. Some reference to adult interest in fairy tales needs to be made, though it is not within the province of this investigation. Even though there is a decline in interest in the fairy tale after the

---

[9]Some confirmation of the general thrust of this explanation can be found in Wolf and Fiske's observation (p. 14 ff) that the oversimplified world of comic book stories with its invincible heros, its improbable situations, and the like, which once held the child's interest, eventually loses its appeal, and in fact becomes the object of intense dislike.

age of 6 to 8, there is a resurgence of interest around the age of 18 to 20 that seems to continue throughout adult life. Proof of such adult interest is not firmly established but is indicated by the popularity of Tolkien's *The Hobbit* (1966a) and *The Lord of the Rings* (1966b), and C. S. Lewis's *The Chronicles of Narnia* (1970). If these are not fairy tales, they possess fairy tale characteristics. Both Tolkien (1964) and Lewis (1966) have mounted lengthy defenses with regard to adults' reading of fairy tales. Also, adults are not unenthusiastic about reading fairy tales to children—which suggests that they themselves receive some pleasure in encountering the tales.

Though further investigation is needed to determine the origins of the adult's interest in the fairy tale, it is possible to speculate. There exist in the tales many more subtle contrasts than the ones referred to earlier in this chapter. Some cases in point are "Hansel and Gretel" (G), where the step-mother in urging the father to abandon the two children is the initiator of evil action, while Hansel by strewing the path with pebbles or crumbs is the initiator of good action; the fire the parents build for the children burns brightly for a while but eventually burns out, just as the parents, after reassuring the children that they will be nearby, eventually slip away out of the forest; a bird leads the children to the witch's house while another one, at the end of the story, leads them home: the first bird was a singing, alluring creature of the dark forest who delivers the children into the witch's trap, while the other was a common duck, a creature of the domestic world who delivers the children to their father and their home. The tales abound in such patterned contrasts and offer many opportunities for noting the craft of the stories, an interest which is more common to adults than to children. But it is doubtful that the above factors could account for more than a part of the adult interest. It may be that the adult's interest in the tale is actually quite similar to the child's. Just as a child seeks identification with a hero who achieves his ends, so does the adult. Just as children seek to deny a confusing real world by entering the more ordered and familiar world of the fairy tale, so do adults who, faced with ambiguities and complexities, seek a similar refuge.

Other possibilities exist. Piaget noted, for instance, that in the adult there are vestiges of animism, magic, moralities of constraint, egocentrism, and the like (1967, p. 234; 1965, p. 262). Though these characteristics, in full panoply in the child, are displaced in the adult by the inexorable processes of development, everyone retains some remnants of these early beliefs which from time to time come to the surface of consciousness and, however fleetingly, reawaken the child in them. Honest adults would admit to finding such experiences pleasurable, but it is the nature of the adult, as Lewis (1966) observed, to feel guilty at the suspicion of being childish (p. 25). But however much these beliefs may cause guilt when they are encountered in the real world, they are not likely to do so when they are encountered in the fairy tale. There they are enclosed in a fictive frame and kept at a distance. And so it may be that adults turn to the tale as the very place where they may encounter and embrace these beliefs with none of the reluctance that attends their experiencing them in real life.

But whatever adult interest there is in the tale, it never achieves the intensity of the child's fascination. That the child's interest should be so intense, however, should come as no surprise. Seeking a respite from the disruption caused by the crisis of experience, children turn to the tale for the world order they once knew and for the satisfaction of experiencing a world in which their magical, animist, moral, and egocentric expectations are fulfilled. At the same time, the controlled form of the fairy tale momentarily renews in children their once unshakable convictions about their parents' power. The fundamental similarities among the tales assure children that the same experience can be had with any tale. And the brevity of the tale enables these gratifications to be achieved swiftly and successively. In short, children, more than adults, are in search of another world more satisfying than their own and find in the tale the world they most seek. The phenomenon of interest produced by this conjunction of the child's mind and the tale's construction is short-lived, but for its duration it reflects children's struggle to establish a relationship between themselves and a world that is as unfamiliar as it is real.

CHAPTER FIVE

SOME IMPLICATIONS FOR TEACHERS, PARENTS, AND RESEARCHERS

It now remains to examine certain of the implications this investigation has for those whose concern is children and books.

Teachers and Parents

Reading the tales: the receiving mode. As indicated in previous chapters, children can come upon fairy tales by independent reading of the tales in basal readers or in trade books—either anthologies or single-tale editions—and by viewing dramatizations of the tales—actual or animated—or by listening to adults read the tales aloud. However, while children show a marked interest in fairy tales at a pre-reading age, the print route to the tales is frequently a difficult one, since most editions of fairy tales are published for a much older group of children who can read the tales by themselves. Certainly, publishers should produce more editions of fairy tales for an earlier reading age. Nonetheless, teachers and parents who respond to the interests of pre-reading age children by reducing the discrepancy between what children want to read and can read should make use of non-print resources. Not only should teachers and parents make use of the dramatizations in modern film and television, they should also read many more fairy tales to children. Reading the tales aloud reinforces the narrative control, those unvarying patterns that suggest both the reassuring limits parents place upon the child's existence and the power that children attribute to their parents. The power of the tales to provide the comfort and reassurance that children seek in the first place is doubled when adults read the stories aloud. By providing children with an experience they can nowhere else have so fully, adults can thus enhance the fundamental appeal of the fairy tale. That also applies to older children. Many teachers and parents will testify to what appears to be the unusual desire of older children to be read to, but, as this investigation has shown, such a desire is a very normal and very important means by which children and even young adolescents can maintain a surer footing in their shifting world.

Adult readers need not be expert storytellers with a repertoire of theatrical gestures and intonations. Even the most subdued narration of a story will work its therapeutic effect, and adults should proceed in the confidence that, in setting aside regular times for reading aloud to a wide spectrum of age groups, they are contributing greatly to the emotional well-being of the children in their audience.

The tale and childhood fears. Regardless by what means the child receives the tale, however, one of the things that teachers and parents always have to confront in bringing children and fairy tales together is the notion that giving fairy tales to children runs the risk of frightening them with the gruesome characters and violent events. The tales do contain such content and some children might be frightened; so the worry cannot be easily dismissed. Frank (1941) responds that children are not so easily frightened as adults may think, and that in fact children enjoy "a dash of horror and a spicing of threat with their stories" (p. 40). But this defense is hardly so satisfying as that of C. S. Lewis (1966), who observes that when it is said that children must not be frightened two things may be meant: one that children should not be given anything that will cause haunting, disabling, pathological fears; and the other that children should be kept from the knowledge that they are born into a world of death, violence, wounds, and the like (p. 31). Given these distinctions, Lewis maintains that it is the children who determine whether an object or experience, *a priori*, has any more potential for producing phobia than does any other. Though Lewis does not put it this way, it is reasonable to assume, therefore, that, while the tale may indeed *occasion* fear, it is not the *cause* of fear. Of the second sort of fears, the natural ones, Lewis maintains that attempts at preventing these produce more harm than good because preventing children from seeing the terrors of the tales precludes their learning the courage that always wars against such terrors, the very thing that makes terror endurable (p. 32).

Lesser (1957) offers an even further defense. When fiction arouses a deep terror, it also encloses the terror in a kind of spatial or temporal frame, reminding the reader that, however powerful and triumphant evil may momentarily appear to be, its dominion is limited (p. 185). For instance, the cruelty of child to parent which prevails in *King Lear* could not be borne if it had gained sway everywhere. Instead it is confined to England; in France, where Cordelia goes for refuge and from which she comes to succor her father, there is a different and more normal world (p. 186).

So too with the fairy tale. Teachers and parents should recognize that however many gruesome characters may lurk in forest or castle, however much violence may swirl about, the tale is set in so distant a time and place that children are assured that they are beyond the reach of the tale's threatening forces. Thus Tolkien (1964) observes that as a child he wished for dragons with a "profound" desire, but he did not want them in his neighborhood intruding into his safe world, and so he turned to reading about them in fairy tales, where he was able to encounter them free from fear (p. 41).

The tale and questionable ethics. Teachers and parents will find that fairy tales are subject to an even further criticism, one regarding the ethical system that promotes their terror and violence. Weekes (1935) indicates that the tales are frequently filled with vindictive kings, jealous mothers, avaricious brothers, and the like and, in addition, often show success as an outcome of deceit and treachery—all of which may lead children to believe that what is depicted is a standard of exemplary adult conduct (p. 163). However, if some child should use the tales as a model of behavior, it may be too facile to ascribe the cause of the child's disorientation to the tale itself. That the child could so easily adopt or want to adopt the behavior of the tale suggests that it is not so much the tale as the child that should be the focus of attention.[1]

The tale and escape from reality. As the present explanation indicates, in the face of the crisis of experience, children need to leave the real world behind and enter temporarily a more stable and familiar world such as that embodied in the tale—in effect, to escape to another world. Teachers and parents will find, however, that any withdrawal from reality has invariably been viewed as pernicious. For example, it is probably not the potential harm to

---

[1]This same sort of causal confusion characterizes Wertham's observations (1954) of children's reading of comics. Coming upon a number of children in his psychiatric practice who were avid readers of comics, Wertham concluded that it was the reading of the comics that was causing the children's disorders. He failed to consider the possibility that the children's reading of the comics was a symptom of their sickness rather than its cause.

the organism that causes the hallucinogenic drugs to be viewed as objectionable but rather their ability to produce an easy escape from the real world. Were potential physical harm the only objection, then an alternative drug culture, one which was completely safe, would answer the objection. But this is not the case, and instead, alternatives *to* the drug culture are sought, those that will keep the individual firmly planted in the real world. The privacy of escape is probably what is seen as most objectionable. Everyone has had the experience of being quietly lost in a reverie while in the presence of others and of not being permitted to continue but instead being snapped back to reality and to participation with the others—sometimes jokingly and sometimes not—by urgings to wake up, to stop daydreaming, and so on. This suspicion of a private, secret life is also to be found in the entire orientation of American psychology, which has generally had a cognitive, behavioristic thrust as Bender and Lipkowitz (1940) and Wolfenstein (1946) have pointed out. Such orientation has viewed any withdrawing from reality as a deterioration and thus a precursor to psychosis, especially schizophrenia.

Of all the objections to fairy tales, the most serious is that they encourage children to retreat from the real world. That objection is especially relevant here, since the present investigation indicates that such a retreat is fundamental to the child's response to fairy tales. The first question is whether the activity of retreat or escape is really so negative as the critics have made it. Although it is true that such activity can reach pathological proportions and can become, as Lorand (1935, 1937) has shown, a permanent pattern, there is much evidence to show that such instances as Lorand describes are extraordinary and that it is normal to seek a temporary release from the real world, whether by reading fairy tales or other means. Bender and Lipkowitz, for instance, show this seeking of escape to be a normal occurrence in the process of development (p. 456 ff); Friedlaender (1942) as well as Lesser shows that a story provides a natural arena in which one's fantasies and wishes achieve fulfillment; and the present investigation shows how inevitable it is that children, in the process of normal development, would seek escape from a world pressing in upon them. Tolkien (1964) offers his own proof when he asks whether it is not natural for a man finding himself in prison to try to get out and go home or, when he cannot do so, to think and talk about topics other than jailers and prison walls (p. 60).

Teachers and parents should also realize that the child's turning to the tale is not only normal, but is profoundly serious. This fact, however, is little recognized or understood. Dalgliesh (1932), for instance, is oblivious to the import of the child's conjunction with the tale when she indicates that to take the tales or the child's reading of them seriously is to destroy their "joy" for children (p. 88). Weekes misses the point when she remarks that reading the tales is a "wandering" through the "colorful" world of unreality (p. 163). Children's turning to the tale is no casual recreation or pleasant diversion; instead, it is an insistent search for an ordered world more satisfying than the real one, a sober striving to deal with the crisis of experience they are undergoing. In such a view, it is even possible, regardless of one's attitude toward bibliotherapy (cf. Shrodes 1960; Alston 1962; Jackson 1962), to see the child's turning to the tale as a salutary utilization of an implicit therapeutic device of the culture. It would appear, moreover, that after reading a fairy tale, the reader invests the real world with the constructs of the world of the tale. Lewis maintained that, after one has encountered enchanted woods in a tale, all real woods become a little enchanted (p. 29 ff). But the tale may not so much change children's conception of the real world as sustain their old conception of it. In the child's conception, characterized as it is by magic, animism, and the like, all woods are, in a sense, enchanted from the very beginning, and so encountering woods in the tale does not so much make all real woods become enchanted as it keeps them from becoming disenchanted. The tale's ability to *sustain* old conceptions in the child is thus different from the tale's ability to *reawaken* such beliefs in the adult. It is comforting to have such old beliefs reaffirmed, such earlier possibilities afforded a longer life, and those who are honest with themselves would attest that more is gained than lost from such a stay. But there is always the fear that children—having embraced the old possibilities, having denied the real world, and having escaped into the world of the fairy tale—will be forever cut off from the real world, never to return, or that they will be forever confused as to which is the true one. In the main, however, teachers and parents should view this fear as groundless; the very fact that children turn from the real world to the world of the fairy tale means that they have recognized a difference between the two. As the present hypothesis has everywhere implied, they have merely made their choice of the one that will satisfy them more.

The choice is made, of course, under what has generally been called the pleasure principle, with all its disregard for the limitations of fact or logic and its immediate gratification of wishes.[2] But the demand for the gratification of wishes does not go unchecked. Under the influence of the reality principle, notions of possibility, probability, and the like—in effect, the pull of reality—prevent a permanent or even a prolonged excursion into pleasure.[3] So the child, having momentarily denied the real world, now denies the unreal one. This shuttling back and forth, this alternating and interacting of the flight from reality and its attendant flight to reality (cf. Searl 1929; Peller 1959), may be a source of pleasure itself, and certainly deserves further investigation, but it can be said that the child's return to reality need not be a reluctant one. Having denied the real world by turning to the tale, the gratifications that the child found were quite literally a respite from the real world, like sleep after a day's labors. As sleep prepares us for the following day, so may the respite provided by the tale prepare the child for a re-encounter with the real world once the story is over.

Teachers and parents will find, however, that objections to the non-reality of the tales persist. There are those who maintain that the tale not only keeps children from reality but actually retards their development—which implies that the child's earliest reading should be less fantastic and more realistic. Those who hold this position of retardation reason that children are more interested in the world of reality than they are in the unknown, unseen world far away in time and space—a conclusion drawn from observing the questions children ask and the things they talk about. Stories of the real world are then seen as a way of furthering the child's acclimation to the world. Realistic stories presumably set up a sense of right relationships between the child and the world, its

---

[2]Under the sway of the pleasure principle, wishes give rise to vivid images of the objects that would satisfy them. The wished-for objects may be, in actuality, difficult, dangerous, or even impossible to attain, but while the pleasure principle remains dominant, there is complete disregard for the limitations of fact and logic. The wish proceeds directly to the imagined possession of its object, and the wish-fulfillment fantasy brings momentary delight. (Freud 1950a, p. 13 ff; Wolfenstein 1944, p. 135).

[3]The physical needs of the organism require physical objects to satisfy them, and so under the necessity of attaining such objects the reality principle is gradually instituted. The imperious demand of the wish is subjected to criticism from the point of view of possibility and prudence, and is also implemented with knowledge of ways and means. The sway of the pleasure principle becomes restricted, and the mere image of the wished for thing is devaluated, paling in comparison with the physical object, while the wish-fulfillment fantasies are criticized as idle dreaming and cease to be the major preoccupation of the waking consciousness. (Freud 1950a, p. 13 ff; Wolfenstein 1944, p. 135).

persons and things, increasing children's ability to interpret their own daily experiences. The reading of fairy tales, on the other hand, would be postponed until children had time to explore the world of reality. It would be only when they had developed the ability to discern relationships, to distinguish between fiction and fact, that they would be permitted to enter the realm of the "remote and the unfamiliar" through the medium of the fairy tale (cf. Weekes, p. 168). More specifically, those who hold this position of retardation take note of children's primitive ways of thinking, that is, their magical and animistic beliefs, and question whether it is wise to let them "roam freely in the world of unreality" that would reinforce children's primitive thinking and retard rather than promote their progress toward logical, realistic thinking. Such advocates insist that the child's first experiences with literature should contribute to the correcting of inaccuracies of thought—as realistic stories would—rather than encouraging inaccuracies, as fairy tales would (cf. Weekes, p. 171).

But the present investigation shows that the children turn to the tale for a temporary denial of a world which is proving all too real for them. And the study implies that the thrusting of realistic stories upon the child is not likely to meet with much success. As children undergo the crisis of experience, they become increasingly aware of what the real world is like. Given the fundamental changes this requires of their conception of the world and the resulting disruption it causes in them, children obviously seek not more reality, but less. In a sense, they require an occasional rest from the struggle of learning about the real world. Stories of reality do not provide this rest and in fact represent a continuation in the fictive world of the very struggle that is occurring in the real world, a compounding of its tensions and stresses, requiring a redoubled effort to adjust. There should be little wonder, therefore, that the child would choose the fairy tale and reject the story of reality.

The child's reading in general. The reality-first view smacks of that pedagogical wish, peculiarly American as Piaget (1967) sees it, to accelerate the child's development. Piaget himself has always admitted that it is certainly possible to accelerate development, but he has also always questioned the advisability of doing so. His hypothesis is that there is a certain optimum learning time for all concepts, and if the rate of learning is too fast the learning will be too fragile; if it is too slow, the ideas will not crystallize. Whatever one's wishes may be, therefore, ultimately it will be the children themselves who will determine the success of attempts to alter development. Attempts to alter the child-determined course of reading interests, for example, are sure to encounter difficulty. In this report and in Friedlaender's investigation of children's interest in stories of reality, children's preferences are strong and unequivocal: when they want fairy tales, they do not want stories of reality; when they want stories of reality, they do not want fairy tales. At each stage, children turn to different kinds of reading to achieve whatever gratification they need. Simply put, children read what they please, or more accurately, what pleases them.

Teachers and parents are understandably concerned, however, with the ostensible instructive value of children's reading and so put before them those books that are thought to be instructive. But this putting of books before children may mean putting them in their way. If children find that reading does not provide the satisfactions they themselves want, they are likely to toss over reading altogether. This, no doubt, is what lies behind that commonly observed phenomenon where, after an initial stage of intense interest in reading, many children become reluctant to have anything more to do with books. Other reasons exist for such a turning from books, but surely adult influence figures importantly. When adult intervention is thought of in terms of culture and literary appreciation, good books or bad, more books or fewer, such intervention is likely to have negative effects. Difficult as it may be, teachers and parents must come to understand that the question is not whether one kind of reading produces a more respectable experience than another but whether it produces a more satisfying experience than another—that is, whether children find in the stories an ever-continuing fulfilling of their own needs and desires.

After reading: the generating mode. After children have been in the receiving mode of reading or hearing a story, they are invariably put into a generating mode, where teachers or parents ask them to make some sort of response, whether by writing or speaking about what has just been read or by producing some creative extension of it through art or drama. The present investigation, however, with its statements about the profoundly serious and intensely private nature of the child's reading of the fairy tale and by implication of the reading act in general, should give teachers and parents pause: they should ask themselves whether children should be moved from the private mode of receiving to the public mode of generating at all, or at least about what the nature of the generating mode should be.

In assessing what it is they expect of children in their public response after private reading, teachers and parents should recognize that if the child, by reading, remedies some of the deficiencies of experience and finds a respite from the anxieties and discontents, dissatisfactions and disillusionments of the real world, then the nature of the generating mode that follows must be congruent. It should deal not merely with cognitive comprehensions about the plot, theme, and characters of a book but rather with affective comprehensions (cf. Harding 1968) about the experience the child has had with the book. Questions asked, whether oral or written, should produce an atmosphere of tentative mutual exploration rather than one where innocence is being tested by maturity. Because of the serious risk that a child may feel that his own unique response is invalid, no question or answer should imply a "right" answer. In trying to enhance the value of the child's reading, parents and teachers should be suspicious of such follow-up activities as making book jackets, participating in a book character parade, or dressing a doll after a character in a book. While these may have their own motivational and instructional value, they also may become ends in themselves and even divert children from the central experience they had with the book. Instead, parents and teachers should do everything they can to enhance that central experience and deepen the understanding the children have had of themselves and their reading.

Clearly, the findings of this report are for adults and not for discussions with children, since the investigation has been aimed toward informing the behavior of teachers and parents as custodians of children's reading.

Researchers

A number of issues for future research arise from the present investigation. Given the relationship between regression and the child's turning to the fairy tale, new research should examine the possibility that regression may occur in the reading of other kinds of stories as well. Also, the suggestion that reading is akin to sleeping should be further explored to determine if there are both psychological and physiological similarities between reading and sleeping/dreaming. Use of Propp's morphology (1968), moreover, may serve as a way to determine to what degree children differentiate among fairy tales and to what degree they see the tales as actually being one story. Studies of older readers' recollections of the tales might be pursued to determine, through the distortions in their recollections, which features of the tales have the most psychic influence. Other research issues certainly exist; two major ones are examined in detail below.

Descriptive and analytic studies. Research in the area of children's reading interests consists of two kinds of studies: descriptive studies, such as those examined in Chapter 1 and Appendix A, which seek to list *what* it is that children are interested in reading, and analytic studies, such as the present investigation, which seek to explain *why* children are interested in a particular kind of reading.

The descriptive studies, while they comprise the most extensively investigated area in the field of children and books, are largely disappointing. After almost three-quarters of a century of research, there still is no study with an exemplary methodology, one which avoids the many problems discussed in Appendix A and in Purves and Beach's comprehensive review of the research (1972). Part of the problem is that any study involving as many variables as are in the phenomenon of reading interest faces many difficulties. But these variables are not so overwhelming as the bewildering procedures and results of the studies of children's reading interests would imply. Rather, the problem is that each piece of research is tossed onto the heap with little real reference to what preceded it or intimations of what might follow. Such disorder in a research area would seldom be acceptable in the sciences, where each piece of research builds upon preceding work and interlocks with other research around it. Considerably better order could exist in the research on children's reading interests if it followed the example of the sciences. Clearly, researchers interested in describing children's reading interests should realize that the greatest service to this reserach area could be performed not by mounting additional studies of children's reading interests but by first establishing a universal methodology—one selecting the best and avoiding the worst of what has gone before, especially with regard to the way reading reservoirs are created and children's expressions of interest are collected. The studies that followed this new methodology would thereby not only be comparable but credible enough to be truly useful to the field of children and books.

The problems that surround the descriptive studies of children's reading interests do not surround the analytic studies, simply be-

cause the analytic studies scarcely exist at all. From the very be-
ginnings of the field of children and books, well-meaning writers
have attempted to answer the question "Why?" by referring to
how particular stories appealed to children's hearts or imagina-
tions. But such explanations are insufficient, and one will look in
vain for systematic, non-impressionistic explanations of why children are interested in this or that type of reading. One reason for
the paucity of analytic studies is that those interested in children's
reading interests are led to believe, when they behold the
plethora of descriptive studies, that research in this area proceeds
solely through the descriptive approach and so adopt it, thereby
compounding this impression for those who follow. Another
reason is that most researchers in the area of children's reading
interests do not have the combined literary and psychological
backgrounds necessary for examining the connection between the
child's mind and the story's construction. Even when they have
sensed that analysis, not description, was needed to answer causal
questions, they have avoided analysis. In some respects, this has
been a blessing, since the avoidance of analytic studies has at least
prevented a thicket of incorrect explanations, which is certainly
less desirable than the existing unenlightening, non-scientific explanations. In any event, the profession needs analytic studies by
researchers with the necessary literary and psychological knowledge. Those already in the field of children's literature should be
more sophisticated. For those about to enter the field, the many
universities with elaborate programs in children's literature
should provide interdisciplinary programs that will produce professionals with the background necessary for an analytic orientation.

When such professionals are trained, the methodology created
for the present investigation, where precise knowledge of the
child and precise knowledge of the book are brought together to
determine how the interaction of child and book produces the
phenomenon of interest, can be tested for its usefulness for other
analytic studies. As these studies come into being, there will be at
last a means of accounting for or predicting the responses of children to books they read. Researchers will then be able to ask and
to answer such questions as "What is it about this particular book
that would cause children of what age and psychological disposition to respond to it in what ways?" or, conversely, "What is it
about children of this particular age and psychological disposition
that would cause them to respond to what books in what ways?"
Answers to these questions would then save all who were con-

cerned with children and books from applauding certain books for children, only to find these works simply ignored or resoundingly rejected by the children themselves. It would also enable the same people to accept with equanimity the tremendous appeal of certain books adult critics reject but children enthusiastically choose.

Describing what children's books are about. Most booklists, whether intended for adults or children, separate titles into content categories. But describing books for children is not as accurate as the ways used to describe books for adults, so the categories for children's books produce only a seeming order and do not really guide book selection. Descriptions of adult books provide useful expectations. Learning that a certain book is a Bildungsroman, the potential adult reader knows that this book will follow the episodes of a hero's life as he becomes educated about the ways of the world. Learning that a novel is picaresque, the adult reader knows that it will also proceed by following the episodes of the hero's life, but that the invariably random episodes generally do not affect the development of the hero. At least one major way of categorizing books for adults is to focus on their events and narrative structure as their distinguishing features, so that they are similar to one another in essential ways. Thus when adults have read a book from, say, the Bildungsroman category, and find it interesting, they can return to that category for another such book with some assurance that this second book will also be to their liking. Moreover, because of the preciseness of the category, adults can familiarize themselves with a vast number of books within a category and quickly become discriminating.

This salutary situation unfortunately does not exist for children's books. Rather than being described in terms of events and narrative structure, children's books are often described in terms of characters. Thus, the presence of a boy hero in a Bildungsroman book for children and the presence of a boy hero in a picaresque book for children cause these two very dissimilar children's books to be placed in the same category—stories about boys. The boy-girl distinction aside, the main result is that children who found one of these books interesting and who wanted another like it would find that the second book was nothing like the first. With fairy tales, children are able to have the same experience again with any tale. Few other categories of children's books are so clearly defined. Children thus may conclude that neither books nor the adults who describe them are very reliable. The exceptions that prove the point are those categories which consist of books-in-series, such as adventures of Nancy Drew or the Hardy boys. These books have held generations of children enthralled, not merely because they deal with some of children's deepest concerns (cf. Favat 1974), but also because they enable children to achieve repeatedly and confidently the pleasurable experiences they seek.

Clearly, the categorization of children's books needs to be fundamentally changed. One approach might be to categorize more often according to their events and narrative structure (cf. Neumeyer 1967), schemata for which could be found in Propp's morphology or in Polti's situations (1912). With its attention to the events of the story rather than to characters, Propp's work provides a model for exploring the possibility that it is the sequences of events and not the characters enmeshed in these events that is the true cause of interest. If this is shown to be the case, then the predicative rather than the nominative features of a book would provide the categorizing focus, with the resulting probability that what adults tell children a book is about would indeed be what children find the book to be about. However, it may really be impossible for anyone but the reader of a book to say what it is about because the content may not exist until the reader, in interaction with it, produces, so to speak, what the book is about (cf. Rosenblatt 1968; Lesser 1957; Holland 1968, 1973, 1975; Bleich 1975). Through very attentive listening to a child's conversation, adults may learn what the child really finds a book to be about. But adults in this situation must be prepared to accept that what the child finds may not be at all what the adult or the booklists say it is. Also, what children say they find a book to be about may be only their conscious awareness and not the reaction of their unconscious.

The greater one's involvement with books and readers, the more one is led, inevitably, to the above unsettling realization. It means that those who guide others who work with children and books will be forever thwarted in their efforts by inevitable inaccuracies and inapplicabilities. These generalizations in turn lead adults into error as they attempt to match children and books, and lead children into disillusionment as they try to find interesting books. Researchers have an important role in discovering ways to determine what a child finds a book to be about, not only so that similar books can be provided for that child, but also so that useful descriptions might be made for selection of books for other children.

One approach might be the use of the techniques of subjective criticism which Bleich (1975) has recently and sensitively formulated. Though the subjective approach is based on the theory that normative responses do not exist and that the book can be viewed only in terms of each individual's response to it, researchers who systematically employed this method with wide varieties of readers and books could eventually develop a reservoir of knowledge about their responses. Such a reservoir would eventually lead to cautious generalizations that would more closely correspond to readers' experiences with books. Such generalizations could be misused, however, to suggest what a "normal," and by extension, a "correct" response would be. But as those who worked with children and books became increasingly aware of the tenets of subjective criticism and of interest as a function of the interaction of reader and book, such a notion would be less likely. Such an approach would increase everyone's awareness of the variety of response and of the importance of making accurate determinations of which factors indeed figure in a particular response. Other books with these same factors could then be provided for the child. Thus, observing that a child is interested in a story about a boy and his horse—whose suffering the boy must end by shooting—the adult may prematurely infer that it is the horse that interests the child and offer a second, seemingly similar book, about a boy who through great effort raises a horse to compete in the county fair, only to have the second book rejected. It was not the presence of the horse, but the issue of separation with its attendant anxieties that had interested the child in the first book. The importance of children's being able to achieve with a second book the same experience they have had with a first cannot be underestimated. Chidren's ability to experience repeatedly the satisfaction of reading is a crucial factor in determining how great the impact of reading will be on their growth and development.

Some adults will question whether children should be permitted to read so many books of one type, thinking there should be a variety so that children will be aware of the full panoply of literature and will be able to read with discernment. However, while wide reading is certainly an important ultimate goal to be achieved over a lifetime, to see it as an objective for children's reading is to misunderstand both the nature of reading interest and the foundations of judgment. As this investigation has shown by reference to the fairy tale, children are interested in certain types of reading at certain stages in their development because they fulfill the needs and desires children have at these stages. If the goal is to permit children to experience how reading can profoundly serve them—and not merely to have them hear adult claims that it can—then we should welcome, not resist, their seeking more books of the same type. Moreover, adults must respond positively to children's impulse to intensive reading not only because it enables children to fulfill their current needs and desires but also because it enables them, through the deep familiarity they achieve with a particular type of book, to exercise judgment and determine which books they find worthy. When children's needs change, and if adults put books before them only after assessing the characteristics of both the children and the books, children will be able to move on to another type of reading. That will, in turn, fulfill their needs and desires at a new stage, where they will become discriminating readers of this new type. If adults will let such a process take its course, it will continue for children, once they have truly experienced it, for the rest of their lives.

BIBLIOGRAPHY

Alston, Edwin F. "Bibliotherapy and Psychotherapy." *Library Trends* 11 (1962):159–76.

Arbuthnot, May H., and Sutherland, Zena. *Children and Books.* 4th ed. Glenview, Ill.: Scott, Foresman, 1972.

Becker, May L. *First Adventures in Reading: Introducing Children to Books.* Rev. ed. Philadelphia: J. B. Lippincott, 1947.

Bender, Lauretta, and Lipkowitz, Harry H. "Hallucinations in Children." *The American Journal of Orthopsychiatry* 10 (1940):471–90.

Bettelheim, Bruno. *The Uses of Enchantment: The Meaning and Importance of Fairy Tales.* New York: Knopf, 1976.

Bleich, David. *Readings and Feelings: An Introduction to Subjective Criticism.* Urbana, Ill.: National Council of Teachers of English, 1975.

Bloom, Harold. "Driving Out Demons." *The New York Review* 23, no. 12 (July 15, 1976):10–12.

Bodkin, Maud. *Archetypal Patterns in Poetry: Psychological Studies of Imagination.* London: Oxford University Press, 1934.

Brereton, Geoffrey, trans. and ed. *The Fairy Tales of Charles Perrault.* Baltimore: Penguin Books, 1957.

Briehl, Marie. "Die Rolle des Märchens in der Kleinkindererziehung." *Zeitschrift für Psychoanalytische Pädagogik* 11 (1937):5–19.

Brown, Kay D., and Krockover, Gerald H. "A Reading Preference Test: Rationale, Development, and Implementation." *Elementary English* 51 (1974):1003–04.

Byers, Loretta. "Pupils' Interests and the Content of Primary Reading Texts." *The Reading Teacher* 17 (1964):227–33.

Cameron, Norman A. *Personality Development and Psychopathology: A Dynamic Approach.* Boston: Houghton Mifflin, 1963.

Campbell, Joseph. *The Hero with a Thousand Faces.* Princeton, N. J.: Princeton University Press, 1968.

Cass, Joan E. *Literature and the Young Child*. London: Longmans, 1967.

Collier, Mary J., and Gaier, Eugene L. "Preferred Childhood Stories of College Women." *The American Imago* 15 (1958):401–10.

———. "The Hero in the Preferred Childhood Stories of College Men." *The American Imago* 16 (1959):177–94.

Dalgliesh, Alice. *First Experiences with Literature*. New York: Charles Scribner's Sons, 1932.

David, Alfred, and David, Mary Elizabeth, eds. *The Twelve Dancing Princesses and Other Tales*. New York: New American Library, 1964.

Dundes, Alan, ed. *The Study of Folklore*. Englewood Cliffs, N. J.: Prentice-Hall, 1965.

Dunn, Fannie W. *Interest Factors in Primary Reading Material*. New York: Teachers College, Columbia University, 1921.

Durkin, Dolores. "Children's Concept of Justice: A Comparison with the Piaget Data." *Child Development* 30 (1959a):59–67.

———. "Children's Concept of Justice: A Further Comparison with the Piaget Data." *Journal of Educational Research* 52 (1959b):252–57.

Eakin, Mary K. *Good Books for Children: A Selection of Outstanding Children's Books Published 1948–61*. Chicago: University of Chicago Press, 1962.

Eaton, Anne T. *Treasure for the Taking: A Book List for Boys and Girls*. Rev. ed. New York: Viking Press, 1957.

Elkind, David, and Flavell, John H., eds. *Studies in Cognitive Development: Essays in Honor of Jean Piaget*. New York: Oxford University Press, 1969.

Favat, F. Andre. "The Application of Psychological Knowledge to the Study of Literature for Children and Adolescents." (ERIC Document #ED 103 906), 1974.

Feeley, Joan T. "Interest Patterns and Media Preferences of Middle-Grade Children." *Elementary English* 51 (1974):1006–08.

Fischer, J. L. "The Sociopsychological Analysis of Folktales." *Current Anthropology* 4 (1963):235–95.

Flavell, John H. *The Developmental Psychology of Jean Piaget.* Princeton, N. J.: Van Nostrand, 1963.

Ford, Robin C., and Koplyay, Janos. "Children's Story Preferences." *The Reading Teacher* 22 (1968):233–37.

Fordham, Michael. *The Life of Childhood.* London: Routledge and Kegan Paul, 1944.

———. *New Developments in Analytical Psychology.* London: Routledge and Kegan Paul, 1957.

Frank, Josette. *What Books for Children?* Garden City, N. Y.: Doubleday, 1941.

Freud, Anna. *The Ego and the Mechanisms of Defence.* Translated by Cecil Baines. New York: International Universities Press, 1952.

Freud, Sigmund. "Formulations Regarding the Two Principles of Mental Functioning." *Collected Papers,* Vol. 4. Translated by Joan Riviere. London: Hogarth Press, 1950a.

———. "Metapsychological Supplement to the Theory of Dreams." *Collected Papers,* Vol. 4. Translated by Joan Riviere. London: Hogarth Press, 1950b.

Friedlaender, Kate. "Children's Books and Their Function in Latency and Prepuberty." *The American Imago* 3 (1942):129–50.

Gosse, Edmund. *Father and Son: Biographical Recollections.* 3d ed. New York: Charles Scribner's Sons, 1908.

Gouin Décarie, Thérèse. *Intelligence and Affectivity in Early Childhood.* Translated by Elisabeth and Lewis Brandt. New York: International Universities Press, 1965.

Groff, Patrick. "Research Critiques." *Elementary English* 47 (1970):651–54.

Hadas, Elizabeth. "The Case for Fairy Tales." *The Children's Bookshelf: A Parents' Guide to Good Books for Boys and Girls Prepared by the Child Study Association of America.* New York: Bantam Books, 1962.

Harding, D. W. "Response to Literature: The Report of the Study Group." *Response to Literature.* Edited by James R. Squire. Urbana, Ill.: National Council of Teachers of English, 1968.

Haugaard, Erik Christian, trans. *Hans Christian Andersen: The Complete Fairy Tales and Stories.* Garden City, N. Y.: Doubleday, 1974.

Hazard, Paul. *Books, Children & Men*. 3d ed. Boston: Horn Book, 1947.

Hoffer, Wilhelm. "Kind und Märchen." *Zeitschrift für Psychoanalytische Pädagogik* 5 (1931):107–11.

Holland, Norman N. *The Dynamics of Literary Response*. New York: Oxford University Press, 1968.

————. *Poems in Persons: An Introduction to the Psychoanalysis of Literature*. New York: Norton, 1973.

————. *5 Readers Reading*. New Haven, Conn.: Yale University Press, 1975.

Huang, I. "Children's Conception of Physical Causality: A Critical Summary." *The Journal of Genetic Psychology* 63 (1943):71–121.

Huang, I., and Lee, H. W. "Experimental Analysis of Child Animism." *The Journal of Genetic Psychology* 66 (1945):69–74.

Huber, Miriam B. *The Influence of Intelligence upon Children's Reading Interests*. New York: Teachers College, Columbia University, 1928.

Jackson, Evalene P. "Bibliotherapy and Reading Guidance: A Tentative Approach to Theory." *Library Trends* 11 (1962):118–26.

Jones, Ernest. "Psychoanalysis and Folklore." *The Study of Folklore*. Edited by Alan Dundes. Englewood Cliffs, N. J.: Prentice-Hall, 1965.

Jordan, Arthur M. *Children's Interests in Reading*. Chapel Hill, N. C.: University of North Carolina Press, 1926.

Jung, Carl G. "Child Development and Education." *The Development of Personality*. Translated by R. F. C. Hull. Vol. 17, *The Collected Works of C. G. Jung*. London: Routledge and Kegan Paul, 1954a.

————. "Introduction to Wickes's *Analyse Der Kinderseele*." *The Development of Personality*. Translated by R. F. C. Hull. Vol. 17, *The Collected Works of C. G. Jung*. London: Routledge and Kegan Paul, 1954b.

————. "Foreword to the Third Edition." *The Development of Personality*. Translated by R. F. C. Hull. Vol. 17, *The Collected Works of C. G. Jung*. London: Routledge and Kegan Paul, 1954c.

——. "The Phenomenology of the Spirit in Fairytales." *The Archetypes and the Collective Unconscious.* 2d ed. Translated by R. F. C. Hull. Vol. 9, Part 1, *The Collected Works of C. G. Jung.* Princeton, N. J.: Princeton University Press, 1968a.

——. "The Psychology of the Child Archetype." *The Archetypes and the Collective Unconscious.* 2d ed. Translated by R. F. C. Hull. Vol. 9, Part 1, *The Collected Works of C. G. Jung.* Princeton, N. J.: Princeton University Press, 1968b.

Jung, Carl G., and Kerényi, C. *Essays on a Science of Mythology: The Myth of the Divine Child and the Mysteries of Eleusis.* New York: Pantheon Books, 1949.

Klingberg, Göte. "The Distinction between Living and Not Living among 7–10–Year–Old Children, with Some Remarks Concerning the So-Called Animism Controversy." *The Journal of Genetic Psychology* 90 (1957):227–38.

Kohlberg, Lawrence, "The Development of Children's Orientations Toward a Moral Order: I. Sequence in the Development of Moral Thought." *Vita Humana* 6 (1963):11–33.

——. "Development of Moral Character and Moral Ideology." *Review of Child Development Research*, Vol. 1. Edited by Martin L. and Lois W. Hoffman. New York: Russell Sage Foundation, 1964.

Kris, Ernst. "Art and Regression." *Transactions of the New York Academy of Sciences*, 2d series, 6 (1944):236–50.

Larrick, Nancy. *A Teacher's Guide to Children's Books.* Columbus, Ohio: Charles E. Merrill, 1960.

Larsen, Svend. "The Life of Hans Christian Andersen." *A Book on the Danish Writer Hans Christian Andersen: His Life and Work.* Edited by Svend Dahl and H. G. Topsøe-Jensen. Translated by W. Glyn Jones. Copenhagen: Det Berlingske Bogtrykkeri, 1955.

Laurendeau, Monique, and Pinard, Adrien. *La pensée Causale: étude génétique et expérimentale.* Paris: Presses Universitaires de France, 1962.

Lesser, Simon O. *Fiction and the Unconscious.* New York: Vintage Books, 1957.

Lewis, C. S. "On Three Ways of Writing for Children." *Of Other Worlds.* Edited by Walter Hooper. New York: Harcourt Brace Jovanovich, 1966.

————. *The Chronicles of Narnia*. Published in 7 volumes (1950–1956). New York: Macmillan, 1970.

Lorand, Sándor. "Fairy Tales and Neurosis." *The Psychoanalytic Quarterly* 4 (1935):234–43.

————. "Fairy Tales, Lilliputian Dreams, and Neurosis." *The American Journal of Orthopsychiatry* 7 (1937):456–64.

Loughran, Robert. "A Pattern of Development in Moral Judgments Made by Adolescents Derived from Piaget's Schema of Its Development in Childhood." *Educational Review* 19 (1967):79–98.

Macculloch, John A. *The Childhood of Fiction: A Study of Folk Tales and Primitive Thought*. New York: E. P. Dutton, 1905.

MacRae, Duncan. "A Test of Piaget's Theories of Moral Development." *Journal of Abnormal and Social Psychology* 49 (1954):14–18.

Murray, M. A., trans. *Carlo Collodi: The Adventures of Pinocchio*. New York: Airmont Publishing, 1966.

Neumeyer, Peter F. "A Structural Approach to the Study of Literature for Children." *Elementary English* 44 (1967):883–87.

Norvell, George W. *What Boys and Girls Like to Read*. Morristown, N. J.: Silver Burdett, 1958.

Olrik, Axel. "Epic Laws of Folk Narrative." *The Study of Folklore*. Edited by Alan Dundes. Englewood Cliffs, N. J.: Prentice-Hall, 1965.

Peller, Lili. "Daydreams and Children's Favorite Books." *The Psychoanalytic Study of the Child*. Vol. 14. New York: International Universities Press, 1959.

Perrault, Charles. *Tales of Mother Goose*. New York: Pierpont Morgan Library, 1956.

Piaget, Jean. *The Language and Thought of the Child*. Translated by Marjorie Gabain. Cleveland, Ohio: World Publishing, 1955.

————. *Judgment and Reasoning in the Child*. Translated by Marjorie Warden. Totowa, N. J.: Littlefield, Adams, 1968.

————. *The Child's Conception of the World*. Translated by Joan and Andrew Tomlinson. Totowa, N. J.: Littlefield, Adams, 1967.

————. *The Moral Judgment of the Child*. Translated by Marjorie Gabain. New York: Free Press, 1965.

————. "Thoughts on Intelligence for the Use of Psychologists and Educators." Lecture delivered at New York University, Washington Square, March 21, 1967.

Polti, Georges. *Les trente-six situations dramatiques*. Paris: Mercure de France, 1912.

Propp, Vladimir. *Morphology of the Folktale*. Translated by Laurence Scott. Austin, Tex.: University of Texas Press, 1968.

Purves, Alan C., and Beach, Richard. *Literature and the Reader*. Urbana, Ill.: National Council of Teachers of English, 1972.

Raglan, Fitz Roy J. H. Somerset. *The Hero: A Study in Tradition, Myth and Drama*. London: Methuen, 1936.

Rankin, Marie. *Children's Interests in Library Books of Fiction*. New York: Teachers College, Columbia University, 1944.

Rogers, Helen, and Robinson, H. Alan. "Reading Interests of First Graders." *Elementary English* 40 (1963):707–11.

Róheim, Geza. "Psycho-Analysis and the Folk-Tale." *The International Journal of Psycho-Analysis* 3 (1922):180–86.

Rosenblatt, Louise M. *Literature as Exploration*. Rev. ed. New York: Noble and Noble, 1968.

Rubow, Paul. "Idea and Form in Hans Christian Andersen's Fairy Tales." *A Book on the Danish Writer Hans Christian Andersen: His Life and Work*. Edited by Svend Dahl and H. G. Topsøe-Jensen. Translated by W. Glyn Jones. Copenhagen: Det Berlingske Bogtrykkeri, 1955.

Russell, Roger W. "Studies in Animism: II. The Development of Animism." *The Journal of Genetic Psychology* 56 (1940):353–66.

Searl, Nina. "The Flight to Reality." *The International Journal of Psycho-Analysis* 10 (1929):280–91.

Shrodes, Caroline. "Bibliotherapy: An Application of Psychoanalytic Theory." *The American Imago* 17 (1960):311–19.

Shumaker, Wayne. *Literature and the Irrational: A Study in Anthropological Backgrounds*. New York: Washington Square Press, 1966.

Sontag, Susan. "Against Interpretation." *Against Interpretation and Other Essays*. New York: Dell Publishing, 1966.

Stern, James, ed. *The Complete Grimm's Fairy Tales*. Translated by Margaret Hunt. New York: Pantheon Books, 1944.

Strauss, Anselm L. "The Animism Controversy: Re-examination of Huang-Lee Data." *The Journal of Genetic Psychology* 78 (1951):105–13.

Terman, Lewis M., and Lima, Margaret. *Children's Reading: A Guide for Parents and Teachers.* 2d ed. New York: D. Appleton, 1931.

Terry, Ann. *Children's Poetry Preferences: A National Survey of Upper Elementary Grades.* Urbana, Ill.: National Council of Teachers of English, 1974.

Thompson, Stith. *The Folktale.* New York: Holt, Rinehart and Winston, 1946.

Thorndike, Robert L. *A Comparative Study of Children's Reading Interests: Based on a Fictitious Annotated Titles Questionnaire.* New York: Teachers College, Columbia University, 1941.

Tolkien, J. R. R. "On Fairy-Stories." *Tree and Leaf.* Boston: Houghton Mifflin, 1964.

———. *The Hobbit: Or, There and Back Again.* New York: Ballantine Books, 1966a.

———. *The Lord of the Rings.* New York: Ballantine Books, 1966b.

Tonnelat, Ernest. *Les contes des frères Grimm: étude sur la composition et le style du recueil des Kinder und Hausmärchen.* Paris: Librairie Armand Colin, 1912.

Uhl, Willis L. *Scientific Determination of the Content of the Elementary School Course in Reading.* (University of Wisconsin Studies in the Social Sciences and History, no. 4) Madison: University of Wisconsin, 1921.

Vries, Jan de. *Heroic Song and Heroic Legend.* London: Oxford University Press, 1963.

Washburne, Carleton, and Vogel, Mabel. *Winnetka Graded Book List.* Chicago: American Library Association, 1926a.

———. "The Winnetka Graded Book List." *The Elementary English Review* 3 (1926b):235–40.

———. "A Reply to the Critics of the Winnetka Graded Book List." *The Elementary English Review* 4 (1927a):6–12.

———. "Supplement to the Winnetka Graded Book List." (Part I) *The Elementary English Review* 4 (1927b):47–52.

———. "Supplement to the Winnetka Graded Book List." (Part II) *The Elementary English Review* 4 (1927c):66–73.

Weekes, Blanche E. *Literature and the Child.* New York: Silver Burdett, 1935.

Werner, Heinz. *Comparative Psychology of Mental Development.* Rev. ed. New York: Follett Publishing, 1948.

Wertham, Frederic. *Seduction of the Innocent.* New York: Rinehart, 1954.

Wolf, Katherine, and Fiske, Marjorie. "The Children Talk About Comics." *Communication Research, 1918–1949.* Edited by Paul Lazarsfeld and Frank N. Stanton, New York: Harper and Brothers, 1949.

Wolfenstein, Martha. "The Reality Principles in Story Preferences of Neurotics and Psychotics." *Character and Personality* (now *The Journal of Personality*) 13 (1944):135–51.

———. "The Impact of a Children's Story on Mothers and Children." *Monographs of the Society for Research in Child Development* 11, no. 1 (1946):1–54.

Zimet, Sara G., and Camp, Bonnie W. "A Comparison Between the Content of Preferred School Library Book Selections Made by Inner-City and Suburban First Grade Students." *Elementary English* 51 (1974):1004–06.

APPENDICES

APPENDIX A

AN EXAMINATION OF SOME DESCRIPTIVE STUDIES
OF CHILDREN'S READING INTERESTS

Of all the areas in the field of children and books, none has been so researched as that of children's reading interests. Yet for all this research effort, there are few reading interest studies that can be pointed to as being exemplary and remarkably few results that can be considered reliable.

Those who would venture to consult or conduct research in children's reading interests must take many factors into consideration, and so the studies examined below have been selected not only for their applicability to the present investigation, but for their usefulness in demonstrating what some of these considerations are.

While the hundreds of descriptive reading interest studies in this century would seem to defy categorizing because of their great variability in design and analysis, there are nevertheless two main characteristics which differentiate them, namely, the method by which the reservoirs of reading materials are constructed, and the method by which children's indications of interest are collected.

The reservoirs in these studies may be either *structured* or *unstructured*. Structured reservoirs are rigidly controlled, invariably being limited to a relatively small number of selections which the investigators themselves have identified and analyzed before presenting them to the children. Unstructured reservoirs are more diffuse, generally consisting of all the books in a particular library or any book the child may have read. Here any analysis of the component characteristics of a selection occurs after the children in the study, by their responses, bring the selection to the attention of the investigators.

Indications of interest may come either from *self-reports* by the children of what in the reservoir interested them, or from *behavioral observations* by the investigators themselves of the children's interaction with the reservoir. With the self-report approach, children indicate their interest by responding to questionnaires or interviews, by naming favorite selections, or by choosing among selections on lists presented to them. The behavioral observation approach involves the investigators' examining library circulation records, performing content analysis of children's free discussion of their reading, or otherwise inferring from children's behavior what their interests are, rather than accepting their self-reports.

Unstructured Reservoirs

The studies with unstructured reservoirs have generally used the self-reports of large numbers of children. Washburne and Vogel, in what became the *Winnetka Graded Book List* (1926a), queried 36,750 children in grades 3 to 10 in thirty-four cities of wide variety in different sections of the United States. Terman and Lima, for their *Children's Reading* (1931), polled 2,000 California children in grades 1 to 8, while Norvell's *What Boys and Girls Like to Read* (1958) was based upon 960,000 expressions of opinion by 24,000 New York State children in grades 3 to 6, and drew upon two other similar assemblies of data which brought the total to approximately 4 million expressions of opinion from 124,000 children.

The reliability of these studies is not necessarily assured by their large populations alone because it is the number of reports per book that determines whether the information gathered is adequate. Terman and Lima did not indicate the number of reports they considered minimal for making a general statement about the reading interests of the whole population, and therefore there is some question as to how much evidence they had in hand to support their statements. Washburne and Vogel required a minimum number of twenty-five reports before including a book on the list, but the sufficiency of this is doubtful, especially in view of Norvell's later computation of the values of 1.5 standard deviations for a varying number of reports. With a minimum number of 300 reports, as in Norvell's own study, 1.5 standard deviations equal 5.1 points, whereas with only 25 reports, 1.5 standard deviations equal 18.75—which underscores the uncertainty of results when only a small number of reports is considered.

The children's testimony is usually secured by means of a ballot or similar device. For Washburne and Vogel, the children were asked to indicate, for each book they had read, which of these expressions most closely described their attitude toward the book: "One of the best books I ever read"; "A good book, I liked it"; "Not so very interesting"; "I don't like it." The children were also asked to tell how easy or difficult the book was to read, and to make a statement on what they liked about the book. Terman and Lima's subjects were asked to indicate on an interest blank those categories of reading, such as travel, history, adventure, poetry, biography, that they "liked" and those that they "liked very much." These children were also asked to name four or five books and magazines they had enjoyed reading during the previous year, and to keep a reading record booklet for the books they read during a period of two months. In addition, the parents and teachers of these children were asked to give information as to how many hours per week each of the children read, and how each compared with others of the same age. In Norvell's study, reading selections which were read and discussed in class, or read in class but not discussed, or chosen and read independently, were ranked by the children as "very interesting," "fairly interesting," or "uninteresting."

The genuineness of self-reports, or course, is always open to question. Given the recognized tendency of children to respond as they think they should respond rather than according to their real attitudes, these studies always run the risk of producing invalid conclusions. Washburne was able to determine that 92 percent of the children were at least *consistent* in their responses in a test, post-test reliability check (p. 27), but other than that, in this study and in the others, the investigators were able to rely only upon the children's good faith in reporting their true feelings, prodding them with such statements as:

> I wish to find out what books children of each age like best, and in order to get the facts I am asking several hundred boys and girls to help me by keeping a record in this notebook of all the books they read . . . . [The resultant list of best liked books] will be of great help to parents and teachers in selecting the books children of each age enjoy most. By keeping this record you will therefore be doing something that will help to make the lives of thousands of children happier. (p. 54)

Some descriptive studies have tried to obviate the problems involved in obtaining true responses by noting children's behavior with books rather than their verbalizations about them. Jordan, in his *Children's Interests in Reading* (1926), used eight public libraries, these in varied sections of New York City, to observe children in their actual reading of books. Though he did not indicate the number of children or books involved in the study, he stated that the method used to determine the popularity index of a book was to

... subtract the average number of copies in [on the shelves], multiplied by two, from the number of copies of each book, and to add one for every eight that had been worn out. In case there were no copies of the books on the shelves, instead of subtracting, to the total number of copies was added two if that number was four or less, and three if more than four. (p. 16)

To this he added a measure of the dirtiness of each particular book's card in the card catalog, plus a report of his observations secured by "slipping around and looking over the shoulders of the children deeply interested in their books" (p. 17).

Jordan did not explain his weighting methods, and the image of his slipping through the libraries, or examining the dirtiness of library cards—those for the author, Altsheler, were "positively black" and so received a "1" rating; Barbour's were not so black, and so received only a "3" (p. 18)—seems somewhat ludicrous. But even though the behavioral observation approach may substitute one research failing for another, that is removing the chance of unreliability in children's responses by introducing the unreliability of the investigators' inferences, it does offer another potentially valuable source of data. Byers, for instance, in her "Pupils' Interests and the Content of Primary Reading Texts" (1964), taped the group discussions of 1,860 first-graders, classified the many topics discussed, and then ranked these topics in the order of frequency discussed by the children.

Rankin, for her *Children's Interests in Library Books of Fiction* (1944), and in her efforts at objectivity, went directly to the circulation records of eight libraries, serving a total of 22,800 children representing large and small urban and village populations in the East and Mid-West. With what seems somewhat more simplicity than Jordan, she computed the probable average yearly circulation per title per copy for each book whose cards passed through the circulation desk procedures. This approach probably does give an accurate indication of children's interest in a particular book, and by generalization, in particular types of books. The possible objection that a book's being signed out by a child does not necessarily mean that he or she will enjoy it has been answered partly by a supplementary study in Washburne and Vogel which showed that children usually go through an inspection procedure before signing out a book; having rejected certain ones in this selection process, they are left with those which for them are potentially the most interesting. Their assessment of a book's interest potential turns out to be fairly accurate: having signed out a book, a child is likely to find it fairly interesting (p. 27).

Even with Rankin's approach, other factors can enter. Jordan notes, for example:

> In many libraries children are permitted to take out two books, but only one must be a story book. Children almost always want to withdraw the greatest possible number, so they take out a story book, then a second book, frequently for no other purpose than that they think they must get everything they can. This causes an enormous circulation of books, which, I am convinced, . . . are not nearly so interesting as the circulation would indicate (p. 3).

The analyses to which the investigators subject the data from these studies are myriad. Washburne and Vogel, although they performed elaborate statistical checks and supplementary studies, ignored the opportunity to draw conclusions from the massive information they collected and limited themselves to the production of a list. The list, however, was not a report of what children liked to read but rather a syllabus of what they should read. Washburne and Vogel gathered a committee of librarians to sift through the list of books the children indicated they liked and to exclude those books which they thought were unsuitable for children to read. In spite of the fact that the librarians did not agree as to which books were suitable and which were not (Washburne and Vogel 1926b, 1927a)—some books classified as being of unusual literary value by some were classified by others as too "trashy" to be included in the list—and even though the librarians unanimously voted as trashy one series of books that was read and liked by 900 children, Washburne and Vogel still held to their principle that books that were considered unsuitable for children, even though widely read, were not to be included in their list.[1]

Terman and Lima also had as one of their purposes the production of a guide to children's reading for teachers, parents, and librarians. Their guiding principle was that wise censorship of children's reading is desirable, and they indicated that they constructed "not so much a list of what children do read, as a list of worthwhile books that children would read if they were given the opportunity to do so" (p. vii). And they echoed Washburne and Vogel in their statement: "We have felt ourselves under no obliga-

---

[1] The list of unsuitable books was available only in mimeographed form from the research office of the Winnetka Public Schools until Washburne and Vogel relented (1927b, 1927c) and published it in *The Elementary English Review*.

tion to include an inferior book simply because children by the thousand have found it interesting" (p. viii). But they did make other uses of their data by ambitiously undertaking and successfully executing a description of the reading interests of children at each age level from before 5 to after 16. Though the description is seldom referred to today, it remains the most systematic and comprehensive of its kind.

Norvell made use of a wide range of statistical procedures, grouping and regrouping his data in order to perform, in addition to the usual supplementary studies of the influences of age, sex, or intelligence on children's reading preferences, further examinations of children's interests in poetry, humor, comic strips, myth and legend, and the like. He also went beyond showing what boys and girls liked to read, for a very large part of his report was devoted to exposing the variance between children's interests and the opinion of Arbuthnot, Hazard, Commager, LaBrant, Hatfield, and others. He indicated, for instance, that the experts praised *Alice in Wonderland* and damned *The Wizard of Oz*, while the children praised *The Wizard* and damned *Alice*.

Both Jordan's and Rankin's studies started out with data that were limited not only in amount but in variety, thus reducing immediately the possibilities for analysis. But they did utilize fully what they had. Jordan selected the most popular author for each of the three categories of interest he discovered and described in detail the characteristics of specific books by that author, speculating as to what characteristics of these books appeal to children. Rankin, having determined the thirty-five most popular books of fiction, selected the first ten and analyzed their literary characteristics as well as their physical make-up, marshalled critical opinion, interviewed children who had read them, and determined what they had in common, in her effort to provide a picture of what books children liked to read.

Structured Reservoirs

Reading interest studies with structured reservoirs, generally using the self-report approach, present a different set of methodological procedures and problems.

Huber, for instance, in her *The Influence of Intelligence upon Children's Reading Interests* (1928), decided upon five selections for each of six types of literature (familiar experience, unusual experience, humor, fancy, information, and heroism and service) and then submitted the selections to seven judges who were asked to indicate how well each selection represented the type of literature under which it was listed, how well it represented the entire field of literature for children, and how difficult it would be for a child to understand the selection.

Dunn, in her *Interest Factors in Primary Reading Material* (1921), selected 243 samples of reading material from 40 different books of primary reading level, and submitted them to 8 judges who graduated the samples from the least to the greatest interest, from the child's viewpoint, producing a list of 31 highest ranking samples of fiction and fact for the reservoir. The 31 samples were then submitted to anywhere from 4 to 11 judges who analyzed them for each of 20 qualities which they felt inhered in the samples, including adultness, animalness, boyness, childness, conversation, familiar experience, fancifulness, girlness, humor, imagery, moralness, narrativeness, plot, poeticalness, realism, repetition, style, surprise, verse form, and liveliness.

Uhl, in his *Scientific Determination of the Content of the Elementary School Course in Reading* (1921), secured reports from 2,253 teachers in 80 cities in 25 states about which primary reader selections proved most successful for use in their particular grade, as indicated by enthusiastic discussion, resultant independent thinking, and requests for re-reading, as well as those which proved most unsatisfactory as indicated by pupils' statements of dislike, difficulty in comprehending, and reluctance in discussing them. Later, 741 teachers in 49 cities in 16 states judged the most often mentioned selections for each of 8 grades from this initial survey for their desirable qualities (about animals, dramatic action, interesting repetition, interesting action, suitability for dramatization, fairy or supernatural, kindness or faithfulness, humor, home life, interesting problems, interesting information) and their undesirable qualities (too mature, hard words, unfamiliar subject matter, abstract or hard symbolism, lacking in action, unreal, too long, scrappy, too sad, too childish, tired of it, monotonous, not told well). From these two preliminary activities, the reservoir of reading material was composed, consisting of those 20 selections most often used in the greatest number of grades and containing what the teacher-judges felt to be the largest variety of appeals, both desirable and undesirable.

One problem that immediately appears concerns the various elements whose existence in a particular selection the judges were to determine. In none of these studies was there any thorough definition of these elements. So it would seem that even the most discriminating and qualified readers would have been hard pressed to make any but the most subjective or idiosyncratic judgments. It is not difficult to determine an element such as verse form or rhyme, but a decision on the elements of style or liveliness is much harder to make. For Huber and for Uhl, the result of this difficulty in making these distinctions is that the reliability of the judgments is not very high. Huber's judges, for instance, differed widely about whether particular selections possessed the indicated qualities (p. 14). Uhl's teachers, though often unanimous about the favorableness or unfavorableness of a selection, had much less agreement as to what qualities made up its favorable or unfavorable character (p. 33). Surprisingly, Dunn reported high reliabilities for most of her judges' decisions, the highest being .992 for verse form, .972 for animalness, with many such as .892 for fancifulness, .885 for moralness, .882 for plot, and so on (p. 31). Such reliability coefficients are high for any correlation, let alone those involving such factors as these. Possibly the reasons for his high correlation were remarkably similar judges or selections with unusually obvious elements or the presence of agreed-upon definitions of the elements they were examining.

In each of these experiments, all the activity to this point was preparatory, that is, establishing and analyzing a reservoir of reading material which could then be presented to the children in the study. Huber's subjects comprised 15 classes in 5 public schools in Yonkers, New York, distributed into 3 equal groups according to I. Q. and time spent in school. The 30 selections were arranged in pairs, in both reverse and natural order, and then read aloud to the children according to a very detailed set of directions with each child indicating by ballot which sample in each pair he or she liked better. Dunn arranged her 31 samples according to certain qualities of likeness and difference existing between sequential specimens:

> It was designed that 1 and 2, 2 and 3, 3 and 4, and so on to 30 and 31 should be paired in the reading to children. In reading 1 and 2 . . . a mythical story about a boy and a story of similar origin about a girl would be compared. When 2 was paired with 3 a girl was the central character in each, but one story was mythical and the other assumed to be historical . . . [etc.] (p. 24)

The pairs were then read to 195 different classes in New York City and 16 schools in Virginia, Arkansas, Missouri, and California, with the children writing on a printed vote slip the key word for the selection in each pair they preferred. About 17,000 individual votes were secured and translated into 601 class-pair votes—the vote of a single class on a single pair—with the median number for any one pair being 412. Uhl presented his 20 selections to 529 children in grades 3 to 8 in 4 elementary schools in different sections of Chicago; they were required to read the selections themselves and pass judgment on each by stating whether they liked or disliked it and by indicating the reasons for their opinion.

In one way or another, these three studies demonstrate how even the most elaborate design for an inquiry into children's reading preferences is a compromise of the various difficulties that surround the task. Both Huber and Dunn obviated the problem presented by the mechanical task of reading by having the selections read aloud to them. But even though they were careful to caution the reader to be as unobtrusive as possible, variables such as rapport with the children and skill in presenting the selection were inevitably introduced, thus raising the probability of lack of uniformity. In Uhl's study, on the other hand, the administrator variable was greatly reduced by having the administrators merely distribute the reading selections and give directions for the silent reading and subsequent judgments. But the independent reading by the children immediately introduces the problem of the mechanical task of reading as a factor influencing the children's responses.

During the analysis of the data from these experiments, problems of design become even more apparent. In Dunn's and Huber's studies there was very little difference between the preference for any one sample over another. In Huber's though the difference between the highest percentage of preference and the lowest was 35.7 percent, the average preference for any one type of selection over that below it was only 7 percent (p. 29). And in Dunn's study the difference between any two samples of consecutive rank was shown to be little more than chance (p. 52). These observed small differences in preference, however, probably do not reflect children's true attitudes outside the experimental situation but instead probably result from the ways the respective reservoirs were constructed. In both cases, the reading material was selected to be in the upper ranges of interest, and so the children were faced with equally attractive alternatives, a choice that would seldom be present outside the experiment. The children did express preferences for certain types over others but, with their preferences being so close to chance occurrences, it is likely that on another occasion the situation might just be reversed. It is strange, therefore, that the investigators did not perform a reliability check of the test, post-test variety on the children's responses, a procedure that under the circumstances seems necessary beyond question.

Uhl avoided the discrepancy between the real and experimental situations, since in his study the children were presented with selections which, in the teachers' opinions, were more or less desirable, the main criterion being a sample's wide use rather than its interest potential.

Another problem that the analysis procedures bring to the surface in these experiments involves the interest factors with which the investigators describe the samples. In Huber, the selections were separated into broad categories, such as fancy or humor, but the grossness of the distinctions meant that a selection could belong to more than one category at the same time: a story might have been fanciful, but it could also have been humorous. Even though a story such as "How the Home Was Built" is assigned by the investigator to the familiar experience category, the story might also fall into the information category. There is thus no way of telling whether a child who voted for this story—which vote would therefore be registered for familiar experience—was not actually voting for it because of its information characteristic. In Dunn, the distinctions among the interest factors were much more precise. A story is characterized not by one term as in Huber's study, but by any combination of the 20 qualities. Such a descriptive procedure better reflects the complex nature of a reading selection and takes into account that a particular piece may be many things at once. As Dunn stated: "A story of a boy may also, and equally be a story of a dog, a narrative, with plot of greater or less merit, lively, abounding in conversation, and withal, pointing an approved moral" (p. 40). The object of Dunn's analysis was to determine the weight of each of these factors as a producer of interest, and she did perform partial correlations of the first order, eliminating in turn each factor from each of the others, thereby producing correlations, for instance, for moralness with animalness eliminated, then moralness with conversation eliminated, then moralness with fancifulness eliminated, and so on.

But the true weight of any one of these characteristics as an interest producer can be determined only by eliminating not one but all of the other factors. For a few of the factors, Dunn indeed performed some partial correlations to the fifth order; that is, she determined the correlation of interest with, for example, animalness after the part that plot, liveliness, fancifulness, surprise, and moralness play in producing that interest have been eliminated. But this partial correlation to the fifth order did not account for the other elements such as conversation or humor which may have been present in the selection but whose influence went unmeasured. And so, though Dunn's correlations did move in the right direction, the analysis was not carried far enough, and to the degree that this analysis was incomplete, so were her findings.

Other problems surround the partial correlation method. In performing some of the fifth order correlations, Dunn found that the correlation of interest with fancifulness after eliminating the share of plot, liveliness, surprise, moralness, and animalness in producing interest was $-.07$ for boys and $+.09$ for girls; after eliminating plot, repetition, surprise, animalness, and liveliness, the correlation was $-.19$ for boys and $-.18$ for girls, which would indicate that fancifulness, in Dunn's words "is at best indifferent and perhaps actually antagonistic to interest" (p. 46). Dunn further concluded that it was the other interest factors which the fairy tales possess—surprise, plot, childness, animalness, or familiar experiences—which caused their appeal and that "true or realistic selections equally possessed of those desirable characteristics would be equally interesting" (p. 47). This conclusion, however, does not seem to be warranted, since it ignores the fact that it is the unique and inextricable combination of fancifulness with these other aspects of true or realistic stories which make the fairy tale what it is. It may be, in fact, that the partial correlation method, with its precise isolating of a factor from all its fellows in a reading selection, is a particularly inappropriate method to be applied to the fairy tale; although the method may measure the influence that fancifulness exerts as an individual producer of interest, it does not measure the influence of that special combination of the elements of fancy and the elements of reality which characterizes the tale. And so, though Dunn admirably showed that it was not fancifulness that caused the appeal of the fairy tale, she probably did not show that fairy tales as a class were not the most interesting of all possible material for primary pupils (p. 49). It is ironic that Dunn's study, more carefully designed and executed than any of the others and employing remarkably sophisticated statistical techniques, should, nevertheless, produce misleading results, while the other studies, because they treated the fairy tale more as a whole, should produce a more accurate indication of children's true attitudes. It is unfortunate, too, that Dunn's study is quoted time and again, as in Weekes (1935, p. 172), whenever support is needed to show that children are not interested in, or should not be given, fairy tales, when, in truth, all that Dunn's study shows is that it is not fancy alone in which children are interested.

In Uhl's study, the matter of interest factors, or in this case, appeals, does not present as many analysis problems—a fact which is probably due to his relatively simple design. The children in the study merely stated whether they liked or disliked a selection and then gave some reasons for their judgment. Uhl reported a number of their responses, but he fails to report his procedures for dealing with these statements. From them, however, he obviously extracted various interest factors or appeals and characterized them with the terms he had used previously with the teachers, in effect performing a content analysis of the children's statements and making his two stores of data comparable. The procedure seems quite reasonable, its subjectiveness notwithstanding, and, as it turned out, successful because the children's comments were frank and serious and innumerable comparisons of teacher and pupil data were possible.

Some recent studies have experimented with a variety of structured reservoirs. Ford and Koplyay in their "Children's Story Preferences" (1968) reported their use of an inventory of 10 pictures in each of 6 categories including blacks, children in general, history, science, fantasy, and animals. The children were asked to circle on each page the one picture that indicated a story they would most like to read and to cross out the picture that indicated a story they did not want to read. The technique of using pictures to represent interest categories, while it does afford an opportunity to determine children's reading interests through a non-verbal instrument, itself introduces a host of problems, mainly that the children may be responding to picture style as much as content, thereby making the inventory a test of picture-style preference and not reading preference. Brown and Krockover, in "A Reading Preference Test: Rationale, Development, and Implementation" (1974), somewhat altered this approach by using the jackets from current children's books, the titles serving as verbal modifiers in place of the black and white pictures of the Ford-Koplyay study. But this technique creates new problems by introducing the additional variables of color and of combined verbal and non-verbal cues.[2] Further analysis of the notion of picture inventories is given

---

[2]It should be noted that this technique of combining verbal and non-verbal factors in a forced-choice situation is not the same as Terry's technique in *Children's Poetry Preferences* (1974) where the forced choices by means of a cartoon character were kept separate from the children's free-response verbal statements.

in Groff's "Research Critiques" (1970), but this approach has yet to be shown to be either valid or reliable.

A potentially more profitable approach will be found in Rogers and Robinson's modest but more acceptable "Reading Interests of First Graders" (1963). The investigators presented the 275 first grade children in the study with 32 questionnaire items such as "a child who is lost," "a haunted house," and "a day at the hospital," representing 4 each in 8 categories such as humorous situations, family activities, and historical events. The children were asked to circle the words "like" or "not like" in response to a written and oral question about each item, "Would you like to read a book about ———?" The major limitation of this study is that the investigators did not take into consideration, as Dunn did in her study, that many of the questionnaire items may have had more than one possible interest factor embedded in them; that is, "a child who is lost" might be of interest because of the child element in it or because of the anxiety element inherent in the notion of being lost. But as with Thorndike's A Comparative Study of Children's Reading Interests (1941), the use of hypothetical book titles or descriptions of hypothetical subjects enables the investigators to create myriad combinations of possible interest elements and then, through factor analysis, to study their separate and combined influence as interest producers.

APPENDIX B

PROPP'S FUNCTIONS OF *DRAMATIS PERSONAE*

The following is a simplified listing of Propp's functions of *dramatis personae* as described in his *Morphology of the Folktale* (1968, p. 25–65). For each function there is given (1) a brief summary of its "essence," as Propp called it, plus (2) an abbreviated definition of the function in one word.

1. One of the members of a family absents himself from home. (Definition: *absentation*.)

2. An interdiction is addressed to the hero. (Definition: *interdiction*.)

3. The interdiction is violated. (Definition: *violation*.)

4. The villain makes an attempt to reconnaissance. (Definition: *reconnaissance*.)

5. The villain receives information about his victim. (Definition: *delivery*.)

6. The villain attempts to deceive his victim in order to take possession of him or his belongings. (Definition: *trickery*.)

7. The victim submits to deception and thereby unwittingly helps his enemy. (Definition: *complicity*.)

8. The villain causes harm or injury to a member of a family. (Definition: *villainy*.)

8a. One member of a family either lacks something or desires to have something. (Definition: *lack*.)

9. Misfortune or lack is made known; the hero is approached with a request or command; he is allowed to go or he is dispatched. (Definition: *mediation, the connective incident*.)

10. The seeker agrees to or decides upon counteraction. (Definition: *beginning counteraction*.)

11. The hero leaves home. (Definition: *departure*.)

12. The hero is tested, interrogated, attacked, etc., which prepares the way for his receiving either a magical agent or helper. (Definition: *the first function of the donor*.)

13. The hero reacts to the actions of the future donor. (Definition: *the hero's reaction*.)

14. The hero acquires the use of a magical agent. (Definition: *provision or receipt of a magical agent*.)

15. The hero is transferred, delivered, or led to the whereabouts of an object of search. (Definition: *spatial transference between two kingdoms, guidance*.)

16. The hero and the villain join in direct combat. (Definition: *struggle*.)

17. The hero is branded. (Definition: *branding, marking*.)

18. The villain is defeated. (Definition: *victory*.)

19. The initial misfortune or lack is liquidated. (Definition: *liquidation*.)

20. The hero returns. (Definition: *return*.)

21. The hero is pursued. (Definition: *pursuit, chase*.)

22. Rescue of the hero from pursuit. (Definition: *rescue*.)

23. The hero, unrecognized, arrives home or in another country. (Definition: *unrecognized arrival*.)

24. A false hero presents unfounded claims. (Definition: *unfounded claims*.)

25. A difficult task is proposed to the hero. (Definition: *difficult task*.)

26. The task is resolved. (Definition: *solution*.)

27. The hero is recognized. (Definition: *recognition*.)

28. The false hero or villain is exposed. (Definition: *exposure*.)

29. The hero is given a new appearance. (Definition: *transfiguration*.)

30. The villain is punished. (Definition: *punishment*.)

31. The hero is married and ascends the throne. (Definition: *wedding*.)

APPENDIX C
SOME NOTES ON THE HISTORICAL ORIGINS OF CERTAIN RECURRENT FAIRY TALE THEMES

Of the many possible ways of viewing the fairy tale, one way is to see it as having actual basis in fact, encapsulating and stabilizing those customs and practices of an earlier age which, though distorted and obscured by time, are nevertheless embedded in the tale.

The Theme of the Youngest Child

One very common theme is that of the youngest son or daughter overcoming the treachery or jealousy of the elder ones and thereby achieving success. The particulars vary from tale to tale, but usually the elder siblings deprive the youngest of the credit that is due him or her and sometimes even his or her inheritance. "Cinderella" (P), (G), "The Fairies" (P), and "The Water of Life" (G) are among the many tales in which this theme may be found. One might say that this theme points to nothing more than certain human traits, such as greed or aggressiveness, which have been given literary expression in this fashion, but such a view does not explain why the expression of these traits in the tales should persistently appear with the theme of the youngest child. A more convincing explanation comes from Macculloch, *The Childhood of Fiction* (1905, p. 351 ff), who notes that once most laws of inheritance were widely based on the notion of *Jungsten-recht* where, if a man died without a widow and left more sons than one, the youngest inherited the lands as sole heir or, if there were no sons, the youngest daughter became the heir. Sometimes the right of the youngest was less marked but still important, and the law allotted to the youngest son or daughter the hearth and an area around it, as well as the best implements.

There are probably a number of reasons for the inheritance laws based upon *Jungsten-recht*. It may have been, for instance, that the youngest orphan was thought to be the least likely to care for

himself or herself; or it may have been that, since the elder
brothers would probably have left the homestead to found new
ones of their own, the father's homestead would logically be reserved for the youngest, who probably had not yet left; or, given
the practice of ancestral worship and its connection with the
hearth and the homestead, it may have been natural that these
rites would fall to the youngest, who was the most likely to still be
at home. *Jungsten-recht*, however, did not enjoy total acceptance,
and it was gradually challenged by the notion of primogeniture.
Elder sons came to claim what they believed was their right and
to oust the now despised youngest son. Macculloch speculates
that it would be to this period that the early forms of the stories of
the youngest child can be ascribed.

As a reflection of the struggle between primogeniture and
Jungsten-recht, these tales picture the youngest child as an ill-
treated simpleton who is the victim of the evil plots perpetrated
by his elder siblings as natural enemies. But the *Jungsten-recht*
still retains its hold, and the youngest ends by overcoming the
wiles of his jealous and treacherous brothers; he comes into his
kingdom after all, and the elders receive their just punishment.
Many other aspects of these stories thus take on meaning they
otherwise lack. For example, the association of the youngest child
with the hearth receives quite literal expression in some tales,
especially those of the "Cinderella" (P), (G) type, where the
youngest daughter must lie among the hearth ashes. So complete
is this association that even her name, *Cucendron* or Cinder-
bottom in the French versions, and *Aschenbrödel* or Ash-stirrer in
the German versions, is derived from the hearth. But where originally the youngest child was looked upon as the favored one, in
the tale he or she is despised; where originally the hearth was a
place of honor, the place of family rites, in the tale it is a place of
degradation. It is easy to see how the conflict surrounding the
concept of *Jungsten-recht* could have produced these changes.
The youngest child became despised and so the youngest child
and the hearth were denigrated in the tale, as literally represented
in the Cinderella type tale. The conflict over *Jungsten-recht* also
accounts for the seeming arbitrariness of the youngest child's
being the subject of the elders' enmity; that is, the youngest has
done no wrong and yet is the object of overwhelming hatred. This
phenomenon may account for the lack of motivation for many occurrences in fairy tales, but more probably reflects that period of
conflicting heirships where the youngest child was despised sim-

ply for being sole heir to the father's estate. No other factor need lay behind the elder siblings' attitude toward the youngest.[1]

Close examination of these tales, moreover, will also show that, just as the youngest child does nothing to deserve the scorn of elders, neither does the youngest usually do anything to deserve the father's estate, although in some tales the youngest child shows gentleness or generosity and is rewarded, and in others the youngest child properly observes ancestral rites of worship and thus becomes worthy of the estate. In the Grimms' version of "Cinderella," for instance, the dutiful young girl plants a hazel twig on her mother's grave, and from this grows the tree that showers down the enabling gifts, rewards for honoring the dead. More often, however, the youngest child seems to have little more than physical beauty to recommend the reward. At first, this appears inconsistent with that fairy tale rule where evil is punished and virtue is rewarded, but consider that the youngest child's seemingly undeserved sole inheritance is a quite literal representation of *Jungsten-recht*, where, in fact, the youngest child did not have to earn reward; it came by right, by law, and not by his or her deeds. In this light, then, such traits as handsomeness, beauty, or unexplained sweetness or goodness can be seen as additional character traits that do not change the plot of the tale and which serve to justify, at least in the world of the tale, the youngest child's receiving the reward.

The Theme of Prohibition

Another common theme is that of prohibition, where dire circumstances follow the violation of a particular interdiction. Stories such as "Bluebeard" (P) are the best known of those tales containing this theme. In these stories, the former wives of a man have been put to death for breaking a command he has delivered, but his current wife, having broken the command also, escapes this fate at the last moment by outwitting the husband and by punishing him with death. Sometimes the husband in these tales is an evil being, and in such cases the former wives, though punished, are usually restored. In others, the person who forbids is not evil,

---

[1]These historical explanations differ greatly from Bettelheim's psychoanalytic explanations (1976) where the youngest child's being the object of his brothers' enmity is a function of a non-specific sibling rivalry, and where the associations with the hearth and its ashes reflect the youngest child's feelings of dirtiness and worthlessness that arise from his guilt about his oedipal desires (p. 237 ff).

and the punishment is evidently just. Curiosity is invariably linked with this theme, and it is often the opening of a certain chamber door that is forbidden. The theme of prohibition can be seen as a moral one showing the fatal effects of curiosity, but Macculloch speculates that it originates in actual religious tabus, the breaking of which resulted in death, the inevitable punishment for encroaching upon sacred things (Macculloch, p. 306 ff). He points out, for instance, that among primitive peoples, the sacred grove, the medicine man's fetish hall, and other such places were not to be rashly approached, since the owner of a fetish or personal spirit incurred danger or loss if someone intruded upon the sacred place.

The original tales of prohibition based on religious tabus, probably served as cautionary stories, showing that violators came to grief. But the religious tabu no longer exists on the surface of these tales, and probably the tale of prohibition gradually became removed from the sphere of religious tabu, and that which was originally the sacred enclosure of the fetish owner became the chamber of the present-day tale; the awesomeness of the original tabu deepened into the horror of the husband's prohibition; the power associated with the fetish owner took on overtones of depravity when associated with the husband; and the punishment originally reserved for that person who violated the prohibition thus became transferred to the person who uttered it.